Praise for Mine The Gaps

I hired Steve for several strategic life science supply chain projects, and he has consistently leveraged the methodology covered in this book with remarkable results. Even though this approach is very structured, it is surprisingly effective in addressing a large variety of supply chain challenges. We have utilized the *Mine the Gaps* framework to achieve many bottom-line and top-line improvements, such as

- ✓ Improving on-time delivery from less than 50% to over 90% within a quarter
- ✓ Improving warehouse storage capacity by 5
- ✓ Reducing order entry backlog by 95%
- ✓ Reducing sales order backlog by 50%
- ✓ Reducing customer order lead times by 50%
- ✓ Reducing materials costs by 4%

It is generally believed that to achieve such transformational results, large investments are required in sexy technology such as AI, control towers, etc. and that it would take a long time to achieve. I can attest to the fact that all this was achieved with precisely zero dollars of capital investment, and many of the improvements were completed within three months. Did I mention that this was also during a pandemic?

As you will find from this book, the approach is surprisingly simple if you follow the framework and don't over complicate your efforts. Obviously, the *Mine the Gaps* framework alone will not be enough. You will still require strong leadership and enthusiastic employees. But now they have a playbook to help guide them on their journey, from selecting a strategic objective to successfully realizing benefits from projects that were intentionally selected to create timely and meaningful impact.

The patients that rely upon the effective management of your supply chain to deliver life-saving equipment and drugs will be grateful that you have taken the time to understand the *Mine the Gaps* system.

(Supply Chain Executive, Global Life Science Market Leading Organization)

Praise for Steve Clarke

"He brought structure to the process and managed a very complex project in an incredibly dynamic environment."

Tobin Schilke, CFO

"I was impressed with Steve's leadership, his attention to detail, his ability to dissect complex problems. Steve did a great job on a very complex project."

Kevin Lundquist CFO

"Steve was instrumental in making the supply chain planning application relevant. He led many projects that optimized Manufacturing, Purchasing, Inventory etc."

Shyam Panda, Founder of Dilytics

"Steve transformed a very manual supply chain into an efficient and system oriented process."

Nicolas Huret, Managing Partner at Chevalier Consulting

MINE
THE
GAPS

M I N E
THE
GAPS

A powerful framework to achieve excellence within
your life science supply chain

Steve Clarke

PYP **Publish**
Your Purpose

For permission requests, write to the publisher, addressed "Attention: Permissions Coordinator," at the address below.

Publish
Your Purpose

Publish Your Purpose
141 Weston Street, #155
Hartford, CT, 06141

The opinions expressed by the Author are not necessarily those held by Publish Your Purpose.

Ordering Information: Quantity sales and special discounts are available on quantity purchases by corporations, associations, and others. For details, contact the publisher at hello@publishyourpurpose.com.

Edited by: Chloë Siennah
Cover design by: Brian White, WG Design Group
Typeset by: Brian White, WG Design Group

Printed in the United States of America.
ISBN: 979-8-88797-054-7 (hardcover)
ISBN: 979-8-88797-055-4 (paperback)
ISBN: 979-8-88797-090-5 (ebook)

Library of Congress Control Number: 2023905365

First edition, May 2023.

The information contained within this book is strictly for informational purposes. The material may include information, products, or services by third parties. As such, the Author and Publisher do not assume responsibility or liability for any third-party material or opinions. The publisher is not responsible for websites (or their content) that are not owned by the publisher. Readers are advised to do their own due diligence when it comes to making decisions.

Publish Your Purpose is a hybrid publisher of non-fiction books. Our authors are thought leaders, experts in their fields, and visionaries paving the way to social change—from food security to anti-racism. We give underrepresented voices power and a stage to share their stories, speak their truth, and impact their communities. Do you have a book idea you would like us to consider publishing? Please visit PublishYourPurpose.com for more information.

M I N E
THE
GAPS

Table of Contents

Mine the Gaps

Chapter 1

Introduction

> *"How would your life be different if you stopped worrying about things you can't control and started focusing on the things you can?"*
>
> **–Steve Maraboli**

A recent medical device client's supply chain was experiencing major challenges. They had grown very quickly, and the reality was that they had outgrown their supply chain capabilities. Senior executives knew that something—or someone—had to change. Sound familiar? I was asked to support their transformation in January, and I am writing this passage six months later, in July. During that time, several key members of the supply chain team left the organization—some jumped, others were pushed. To make matters worse, the global supply chain environment became a "hot mess." (No need for me to regurgitate all the disruptions since they are well documented, and supply chain leaders are all too familiar with them.) Given those circumstances, it would be forgivable if supply chain performance suffered or, at best, maintained its historical performance, right?

However, if I told you that their on-time shipping performance actually improved from 45% to 86% during this period, you'd probably want to learn more about how we accomplished that. If I also told you that this was achieved with no capital expenditure and no technology investments, you would be even more curious about how we did it. And if you knew that we uncovered the key reasons for their performance issues and had an action plan in place to quickly address them within a 90-minute workshop, you would be excited to learn what approach turned things around. While their supply chain had been underperforming for many years, they had the data at their fingertips all along—they just had to use it.

I often hear that this approach won't work in a particular environment because most issues are "out of their control." While it's true that no approach can magically free up a container delayed at the Long Beach port, in my experience, most late order issues actually *are* within your control. **And the more issues that are out of your control, the more critical it is to address those within your control—the *gaps*.** At the medical device client described earlier, they were surprised to find that over 50% of their late orders could have shipped on time. Multiple order management-related issues—*gaps* within their control—prevented on-time shipment. Though it had been a problem for years, this was a revelation to the operations team. (You may be thinking this was just a fluke but believe me, it is not!) Using my unique framework, I have resolved these issues successfully for several life science organizations as well as companies in other industries.

As you may have guessed from the title of the book, I have named the framework *Mine the Gaps* because that is exactly what we do. The beauty of this approach is that it is not limited to improving on-time shipments. In fact, almost every imaginable supply chain objective can be addressed using *Mine the Gaps*. I have used it multiple times over the years to achieve other strategic objectives such as inventory turns improvement, excess inventory reduction, improved warehouse space utilization, logistics cost reduction, scrap reduction and inventory accuracy. I cover most of these cases later in the book. Do I have your attention yet? If so, read on!

In the following chapters, I will introduce you to the *Mine the Gaps* framework, which has repeatedly achieved transformational results. You will learn how to uncover gaps in performance, processes, technology, etc., and then address them. You may be asking yourself "Why do I need a framework?" Like all things in the supply chain, the devil is in the details. Here are some questions that my framework will help you answer:

> ➤ **How do we align our organization?** Which steps should we take, and in what sequence to achieve strategic objectives such as "delivering the perfect order"? How do we prioritize projects to achieve these objectives? Which are the "A" projects that we should focus on, and which are the "C" projects we should stop immediately?

➤ **How do we effectively measure success?** Which metrics should we select? How do we make metrics a force for good, not something to be feared? How do we select metrics that encourage different functions to collaborate towards a common goal?

➤ **How do we find quick wins?** Most organizations are impatient for improvements, which often causes them to do counterproductive things to meet their quarterly goals. At the same time, they are often wasting resources on worthless projects. Instead, using this approach, we will collect data that is almost always at our fingertips and perform a structured analysis to find quick wins. This approach will allow time to sustainably build your supply chain for the long-term.

➤ **Where do we find the gaps?** Where are the gaps hiding? What data should we be looking at, and what data should we ignore? The gaps can be found using several techniques, but it is important to know which sequence to leverage them effectively.

➤ **How do we transform how work gets done?** Some of the gaps can be found by analyzing and redesigning business processes. But there are countless business processes, so how do we choose? Which part of the process should we focus on? How do we systematically assess the process to effectively achieve our strategic objectives?

➤ **How do we build long-term capability?** I have developed a supply chain capability model that helps organizations assess their current capabilities across multiple domains, such as people development, supply chain business processes and best practices, data, technology, metrics and Lean. This will guide you on how to build a realistic road map that is tailored to your specific needs and prioritized based upon your strategic objectives.

➤ **How do we realize value from our projects?** Most projects fail to meet their objectives. Even if you have followed the *Mine the Gaps* framework exactly so far, you must execute the project that was meant to close the gap, or you'll be disappointed with the final results. In addition to being ineffective, many projects are late or take much too long to complete. How can we get these projects completed in a fraction of the normal time?

Focus on the "Critical Few" and Ignore the "Trivial Many" Tools

In my 25+ year career leading strategic supply chain initiatives, the one thing that stands out above all else is the amount of people's time and energy that is wasted performing unnecessary work that is unreasonably complicated. During my career, I have noticed that a few tools and practices can very effectively address this waste and complexity. In fact, I have successfully leveraged the same tools, time and time again. These few tools come from several disciplines: supply chain management, Lean Six Sigma, business process management, project management, performance management, and system capability development.

Because I'm a geek when it comes to learning about these disciplines, I have pursued formal training in them all and practice them regularly. What I have found, however, is that I did not utilize the majority of what I learned in various certification programs: Certified Production and Inventory Management, Certified Supply Chain Professional, Lean Six Sigma Black Belt certificate, Certified Project Manager, Strategic Supply Chain Management certificate, etc. To satisfy myself that this was true, I reviewed the Table of Contents for several course manuals. I found that, indeed, I only utilized a small portion of the total practices. Since I have worked in the full spectrum of supply chain functions in multiple industries from an entry level planner to the Senior Global Supply Chain Director, I am confident that if I haven't needed a tool by now, it is unlikely that it's useful in practice.

The *Mine the Gap* framework below leverages the "critical few" tools that will have the greatest positive impact on your organization, rather than wasting your efforts trying to identify them yourself among the "trivial many" tools.

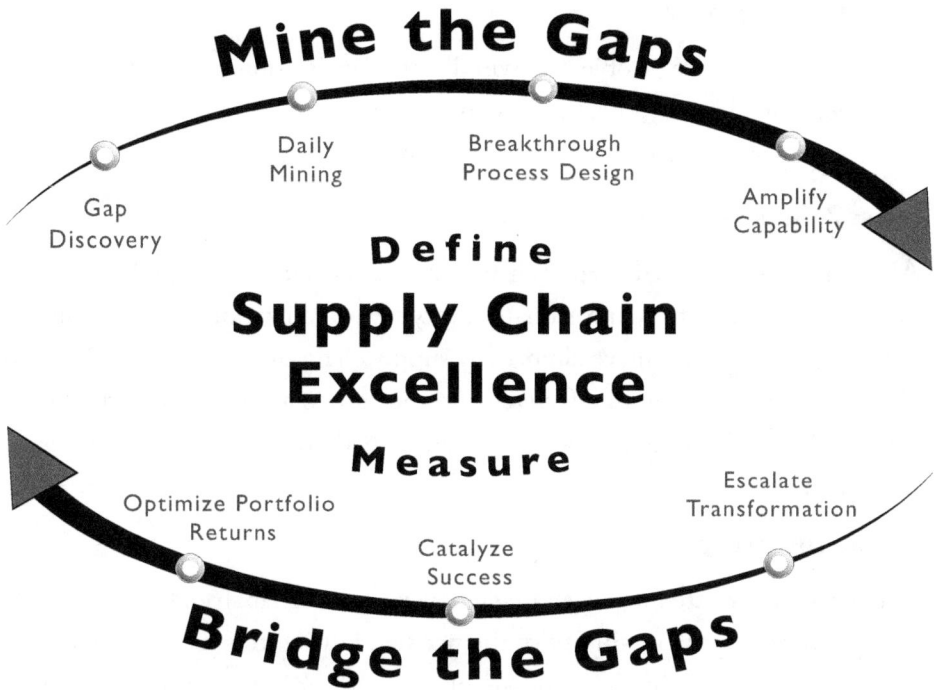

Mine the Gaps

Gap Discovery · Daily Mining · Breakthrough Process Design · Amplify Capability

Define Supply Chain Excellence Measure

Optimize Portfolio Returns · Catalyze Success · Escalate Transformation

Bridge the Gaps

Here is an Explanation of Each Step of the Framework:

PHASE 1: SUPPLY CHAIN EXCELLENCE

Regardless of the company, all supply chains have the same general objective, which is to be able to deliver the perfect profitable order consistently and sustainably. The purpose of all the projects, scorecards, technologies, meetings, employees, etc., is to simply just make that happen. There are two stages at this phase:

Define Excellence

If we break down "perfect profitable order," you will notice that there are two elements to it—customer service (perfect order) and cost (profitable order). Generally, the supply chain costs within a life science company are relatively low as a percentage of revenue, so customer service is often the focus. Regardless, having a clear picture of your strategic objective is imperative. Your organization must be aligned on this point.

Measure Excellence

Your selected strategic objective will direct your decision on which metric(s) to select. In addition, a healthy system is required to avoid the many pitfalls commonly associated with performance management.

PHASE 2: MINE THE GAPS

All organizations have data at their fingertips that can be leveraged to solve their most chronic issues. But, unfortunately, very few organizations use it. By using selected data, we can achieve almost any supply chain objective. In this book, you will learn how and when to effectively use the data to achieve transformational results quickly with minimal capital investment. There are four stages at this phase:

1. Gap Discovery

"Defect data" related to the strategic objective can be analyzed to identify the only critical gaps that will "move the needle." During this discovery phase, Gap Discovery will use simple problem-solving tools. Your team can easily learn these tools and immediately become effective problem-solvers.

2. Daily Mining

Daily supply chain disruptions are a reality of life. Daily Mining will help you minimize the impact of these disruptions by developing a structured, daily process. This will keep everyone aligned and ensure the supply chain status is very visible across your organization.

3. Breakthrough Process Design

Solid supply chain performance results require good people and robust business processes. Breakthrough Process Design uses seven principles of business process redesign to radically improve how work gets done. This will minimize pain points, cross-functional disconnects and transform your supply chain performance.

4. Amplify Capability

Leveraging my proprietary supply chain capability model, Amplify Capability will perform a holistic assessment across multiple domains. These domains include people, processes, and technology. This assessment can be used to help build a strategic road map prioritized to your needs.

PHASE 3: BRIDGE THE GAPS

The Bridge the Gaps phase will help prioritize the gaps to achieve "quick wins" and develop a holistic roadmap that will address your more challenging gaps.

There are three stages in this Bridging the Gap phase:

1. Escalate Transformation

As we identify gaps, solutions will be prioritized with a simple, data-driven, structured approach. The "low-hanging fruit" can be picked immediately to create quick wins, which will help develop your credibility and buy some time to address more long-term solutions.

2. Catalyze Success

Wherever possible, the power of kaizen events can be leveraged to make rapid progress using empowered team members. Successful events will result in radical improvements in lead times, inventory, on-time delivery, costs, etc.

3. Optimize Portfolio Returns

Effective project portfolio management using a data-driven, structured approach will ensure that projects are properly and consistently selected and prioritized. In addition, you will consistently realize benefits through effective project management. In other words, we do the right things, right!

By utilizing the *Mine the Gaps* framework, your team will start to think differently about how to solve problems. In time, this way of thinking will become second nature and you will have a team of highly capable problem-solvers. But, more importantly, they will be solving the problems most critical to your organization: the problems that are blocking your ability to meet your strategic objectives.

Swimming Upstream

Although this framework can be utilized in any industry, this book is focused on life sciences, because that is where I have gained most of my experience, and my anecdotes are primarily from this sector.

The waste and complexity to which I was referring earlier is amplified in highly regulated industries such as life sciences. In many of these organizations, well-meaning professionals insist upon the most conservative interpretations of the innumerable regulations that we must all live by these days. For example, operational work instructions that are rejected because the reviewer from QA found a grammatical error. Better still, how about when black ink is the only color that can be used to fill out a batch record? Or the date must be in a very specific format, or it will be firmly rejected? It is often so difficult to make changes to a procedure that only the most passionate and motivated change agent has the energy to make it happen. (Unfortunately, that person was often me, which I swear was a large contributor to my premature baldness.) Although it took many people to agree to make any change, it only took one person to say "no" for the entire initiative to die on the vine. I truly believe that for some people, "no" is the only word in their vocabulary.

Even if the change was agreed to, the amount of documentation to be updated was endless impact assessments, change requests, validation requests, training curricula updates, training assignment updates, training material approvals, training instructor approvals, instructor-led training, online training, on-the-job training, and on and on and on. Did I mention that this drove me nuts?

In all seriousness, what these well-meaning naysayers do not realize is that stymieing peoples' creativity and initiative is very counterproductive. Isn't the purpose of these regulations to improve the quality of the product and processes? Unfortunately, somewhere along the way, the intent was lost, and the regulations have become a self-perpetuating bureaucracy. The bottom-line result to the organization is unnecessary delays and unrealized objectives and, quite often, discouraged, frustrated employees.

At times, it seems that these organizations are willfully making their operations more complicated than they need to be, which never ends well. It is a vicious cycle where complexity causes mistakes, so more controls are added to mitigate that specific risk, but this creates more complexity causing other mistakes, and so on.

This unhealthy approach and its impact on employees are not restricted to any organizational level. Unfortunately, it infects everyone from the shop-floor employee to top executives; in other words, waste is everywhere. On the shop floor, that could mean filling out documents that you know will never be seen by another human being. In middle management, it's spending hours collecting data every month for a metric to populate a scorecard that nobody will act upon. For example, at one life science company, I participated in the quarterly quality management review ritual (required by the FDA) where quality-related metrics were reviewed with the appropriate level of seriousness. It was obvious that the metrics had been performing poorly for many, many quarters, and it was equally obvious that nothing was ever done about it. I suggested that we not update the scorecard until action had been taken on the poorly performing metrics from the previous update. After all, it took lots of time and energy to collect the data and put together beautiful-looking slides. As you might imagine, this proposal was treated with the disdain that it apparently deserved. Obviously, we couldn't not publish these metrics and hold the quarterly meeting because the FDA expected it, and besides it stated quite clearly in the SOP that this is what we do. I was about to state the blindingly obvious that I'm sure the FDA would prefer that we resolve these quality issues, rather than reviewing slides and nodding heads, with the occasional frown. But I realized that this would fall on deaf ears, so I bit my tongue.

As we continue up the corporate ladder, the waste does not get any better, just more expensive. Executives are forced to participate in, or force their employees to participate in, many unproductive meetings. The quality management manual states that it is a good practice to have 1:1 meetings with direct reports every week, staff meetings once per week, town hall meetings once a quarter, and so on.

Executives now spend an average of 23 hours per week in meetings, up from less than 10 hours in the 1960s. They also report that only about 17% of meetings are generally productive and efficient.[1]

Enough, Already!

As I mentioned earlier, after 25+ years in senior management positions, having experienced this frustration in both large and small organizations, I felt compelled to write this book. I hope to save companies and people from wasting time and energy by providing a little knowledge based on my experience. And the best part is it's relatively easy! All it takes is a little training mixed with skill and determination, and soon enough organizations can navigate around these frustrations toward rapid, successful transformation. Of course, I don't pretend to have all the answers. All I can say is that the practices and tools that I share in this book have consistently served me well and helped me successfully deliver on strategic projects in multiple organizations, large and small, in a variety of industries.

This framework will guide your journey to supply chain excellence. It provides guidance in terms of **what to do and when to do it**, which is helpful, but this book will also show you **how to follow each step**. I will highlight the pitfalls to avoid and describe examples of how I have successfully leveraged each practice throughout my career. Toward the end of the book there are two chapters committed to a full case study including a step-by-step description of how I leveraged these tools to transform the on-time delivery performance of two life science clients.

---

1   Source: https://hbr.org/2017/07/stop-the-meeting-madness.

Chapter 2

Phase 1:
Define and Measure Supply Chain Excellence

> *"What gets measured gets done, what gets measured and fed back gets done well, what gets rewarded gets repeated."*
>
> **–John E. Jones**

I took a summer job after I graduated college in a soda bottling plant. Because of my science background, I worked in the Quality Control lab testing products off the production line. Occasionally there would be a bad batch that needed to be quarantined. One day, I took this action and put a label on the pallets clearly indicating their status. The day happened to be the last day of the quarter, so failing a batch was not good news, as the plant had shipment quotas to meet. So, guess what happened? Yep, the plant manager chose to ignore the fact that the soda was flat and shipped the batch out anyway.

At another organization, to hit their monthly inventory targets, the warehouse operators were told to turn away supplier deliveries or reschedule them to the following month, thus creating potential line down shortages, demurrage costs, and ill will with the customers. All so someone up the chain could get their bonus and receive kudos at the next management meeting. I'm quite sure if you have worked in the corporate world for some time, you will not be surprised by this behavior. Given that metrics systems are so often dysfunctional, why does almost every organization still have them?

The answer is that measuring performance seems to be a perfectly sensible activity, right? We wouldn't not measure it in our personal life. We try to be on time. We try to watch the bathroom scale and we measure how far we jog, even if it's just around the block. We measure the speed at which we are driving (at least some do), how much gas is left in the tank, our bank balance, and so on. In short, if we didn't use metrics, we would be lost, our health would be at risk, our finances would be in shambles and, eventually, we would end up in jail.

Very few topics in corporate life are more divisive than metrics. "If you asked Peter Drucker (the management guru), he would tell you that, "What's measured improves." On the other hand, others will tell you that metrics are a modern scourge that must be removed from the face of the earth. As stated by Jerry Z. Muller in *The Tyranny of Metrics*, "Metric fixation leads to a diversion of resources away from frontline producers toward managers, administrators, and those who gather and manipulate data."

As always, the truth is somewhere in the middle. Done correctly, metrics can be a very powerful force for good. Unfortunately, I have not seen much evidence of this. Instead, I have mostly seen how metrics make smart people do dumb things. It is the execution of the performance management system that is almost always at fault. Here are some questions that we will answer in this chapter to help dodge the minefields waiting for you in performance management:

➤ **How do we integrate objectives and metrics across the organization to avoid each department focusing only on its own objectives?**

➤ **Even if we hit the targets set for all our metrics, does that mean we will have performed in the customer's eyes?**

➤ **When should we take action when targets are not met and when should we pause, rather than spending energy on something that is not really broken?**

➤ **If we do act, how do we decide which action to take?**

➤ **Why should we hold off on leveraging technology?**

In this chapter, we are going to focus on metrics. At a high level, every supply chain has the same objective, that is to simply deliver a profitable perfect order. We all know that it is much easier said than done, but starting with the end in mind enables us to focus our attention on what's most important. Most organizations have a multitude of metrics but, in the end, if we can't see how each metric impacts our ability to ship the perfect order or how it impacts profitability, then its value is questionable.

Integration

Supply chain organizations all too often continue to operate in silos. Even before the concept of a supply chain existed, companies had the functions of procurement, manufacturing, and logistics, and each had its own metrics. When companies pulled those functions together and called them a "supply chain," often they didn't step back and design a bespoke set of metrics. They just continued using all the functional metrics they already had. However, everything in the supply chain is interconnected; have you ever played whack-a-mole? When you push down in one area, something pops up in another. But most organizations do not have one integrated measurement system, which leads to sub-optimization. This is the practice of focusing on, or making changes to, one component of a total system without consideration of the impact overall. Measuring pieces of an interrelated system separately will always lead to sub-optimization.

Measures must be aligned with strategy, and then integrated across the entire organization. There are two types of measurement integration: vertical and horizontal. Vertical integration involves the connection between strategy and measures through different levels of the organization. Horizontal integration is the connection of measures across organizational functions and processes. Organizations should be focused on the performance of the whole, not the independent performance of the parts. Think of how a sports team functions optimally: if all the players are just trying to maximize their individual performances and stats, it will not lead to a cohesive whole.

The key is to first determine the desired outcomes of the organization, identify the drivers of these outcomes, then demonstrate their relationship to your teams. In other words, create *Line of Sight (LOS)*. LOS describes one of the most important concepts in performance measurement. It refers to the ability of employees at all levels to see how their work and performance measures relate to the work and performance measures of others, and to organizational success. Rather than starting with all the detailed functional metrics and trying to make sense of them, start with the outcome and work your way back through the supply chain in increasing levels of detail.

Instead of functional metrics, identify key drivers that enable the perfect profitable order, which will then help your organization select measurements that are most relevant. In the life science space, there is a bias toward wanting to achieve the perfect order, rather than minimizing costs. That is because, in general, profit margins in life sciences tend to be relatively large compared to other industries. Therefore, it is more important to ensure that the product gets to the customer on time and in good condition. This is true even if it means spending more to make it happen. Therefore, for the remainder of this chapter, I'm going to assume that the strategic objective is achieving the perfect order.

Voice of the Customer (VOC)

From a customer's perspective, they want to receive what they want, when they want it, in full, and in perfect condition. Often, companies in early stages of maturity are not able to measure that level of detail. Frequently, they can measure something like what percent of customer orders they were able to ship versus the customer request date or the manufacturers' commit date. However, it does not measure whether an order was accurate or in perfect condition, or whether it was delivered to the customer when the customer wanted it.

As companies mature and implement new technologies, they may evolve the service metric from on-time shipment (Did we ship it on time?); to on-time delivery (Did the customer receive it on time?); then to a perfect order (Did the customer receive an order that was complete, accurate, on time, and in perfect condition?). This is obviously much better than just measuring on-time shipment, since there is much more to satisfying the customer than merely shipping on time.

I have also found that many companies give themselves all kinds of exclusions in their service metric calculations. They might not include backorders or orders requested with a short lead time. While this may be convenient for the company, it isn't useful if you haven't asked the customer what is important to them. Many times, when you do talk to the customer, you find out they don't care about what you're measuring but are much more concerned with another metric entirely.

A simple way to align service metrics is for each company in a supply chain to ask its customers, "How do you measure the performance of your suppliers?" With that information, the suppliers can adopt those metrics as their own. When you and your suppliers look at the same metrics, it becomes much easier to collaborate on improvements that will benefit everyone.

Level 1 and 2 Metrics

Level 1 metrics are the ones that measure the overall desired outcome of a particular supply chain. For example, service levels need to be 99.2%, at margins of 25% of revenue. Level 2 metrics are the key drivers that impact Level 1 metrics. For example, if on-time delivery is your Level 1 metric, then forecast accuracy could be a Level 2 metric.

A Word of Caution

Unfortunately, the measurement systems within most organizations are terrible. Michael Hammer, author of *Reengineering the Corporation: A Manifesto for Business Revolution*, put it this way: "A company's measurement systems typically deliver a blizzard of nearly meaningless data that quantifies practically everything in sight, no matter how unimportant; that is devoid of any particular rhyme or reason; that is so voluminous as to be unusable; that is delivered so late as to be virtually useless; that it languishes in printouts and briefing books, without being put to any significant purpose… In short, measurement is a mess."

You are probably familiar with examples of where seemingly smart managers have felt compelled to do really dumb things to meet metric targets, such as:

➤ **Revenue Targets**
  ◆ Sales managers who alienate key customers because they need to close a sale by the end of the month to get their quarterly sales bonus.
  ◆ Plant employees that ship products before customers' desired delivery dates to make their numbers.

- Companies that ship incomplete orders to make critical on-time delivery dates or sacrifice one very important late shipment for the sake of others that might be delivered on time.

- Salespeople who delay processing orders if they have already made their quota, so they can have an additional sale in the next period.

➤ Inventory Targets

- Plants that refuse to receive shipments of raw materials at the end of each month, so that month-end inventory targets will be met—even if production suffers and customer orders are not filled.

- Companies that rotate inventories to various plants just before audits to make it appear that inventory levels are appropriate—when they really aren't.

➤ Safety

- Employees who under-report (and even hide) accident data to improve "accident-free days" or "lack of recordable incidents" metrics rather than being encouraged to find out what happened and thereby reduce future accidents.

➤ On-time Delivery

- To attain rewards, a company adopts a measure of on-time delivery that only reflects whether the product leaves its plant on time, rather than if it arrives to the customer on time. It measures a near-perfect delivery record, yet some 50% of customers complain that their products arrive late.

➤ Cost Reduction

- Purchasing departments that are measured and rewarded on price discounts negotiated, even if production is stuck with huge inventory. Unfortunately, no one is measuring the cash flow that is eaten up by the inventory, the space it takes up, the maintenance it requires, or that much of it is ultimately written off as waste.

- Many companies refuse to write off excess and obsolete inventory, since it will impact the bottom line. As a result, it sits gathering dust in the warehouse.

Why would organizations continue to do dumb things like the examples above? One primary reason is that executives are oblivious to the harm their approach does to everyone else within the company. They typically create too strong a link between measurement and reward. In this environment, metrics are seen as a negative force instead of a force for good. Since people inherently do not like to be judged, it is important to make a point of separating judgment from measurement within your enterprise. Do people feel the need to "game" the metrics instead of seeing them as a tool to help improve the business? If so, that's an indication that metrics are seen as a tool for judgment rather than improvement.

You might wonder how to improve if people are not held accountable for their results. The key is to enquire about what is being done to improve performance: What is the quality of their corrective actions? Have they defined the problem accurately and concisely? Have they obtained the appropriate data to analyze failures? How have they prioritized their actions?

Ultimately, this is how performance improves in a more functional way.

Example: Large Medical Device Manufacturer

In the supply chain organization of a large medical device client, I discovered that measurements were in place but were very ineffective. Their primary purpose was to check a box for when the FDA knocked on the door. Aside from that, I did not find evidence that the metrics were adding much value. Worse still, since they were being used to judge people, each manager set their target levels low enough, so they were easily achieved. This way, they received a pat on the back at the end of each month. This is what I refer to as a "conspiracy to mediocrity." In this environment, mediocre performance is almost inevitable.

To minimize this dysfunctional behavior, I worked with the supply chain team to see their current targets as the minimum acceptable performance level. Then, we set stretch targets and removed fear around missing these targets. In effect, **we focused on the ceiling instead of the floor.**

In our regular meetings, I consistently asked the following questions when improvements were constrained by a specific issue:

➤ **What was the root cause?**

➤ **What can we do differently to improve performance?**

➤ **What is the action plan?**

I made it clear that not achieving the stretch target was acceptable; not having a plan to continually move in the direction of the stretch target was unacceptable. Slowly but surely, performance improved across multiple dimensions including on time delivery, material costs, and inventory turns. Eventually the "floor" was no longer needed since performance had improved far beyond this level.

Distorting the Data

In companies where people believe they need to always show good numbers there is endless debate over the accuracy of the numbers and what they mean. I'd rather stick needles in my eyes than listen to another one! (Those of you that have sat through those debates will know what I'm talking about.) The result is "analysis paralysis"—an inability to move forward and take the steps needed to continually improve business operations.

In a culture of positive measurement, there is no motivation to cheat; whereas in a negative one, there are always motives to manipulate the flaws in the system. As Brian Joiner wrote in *Fourth Generation Management*, there are three main choices: distort the data, distort the system, or improve the system.

Maybe the most egregious example of this principle in my experience was a client that continued to encourage customers to place orders out into the future. The goal was to make their order backlog increase to impress investors with the popularity of their products. On the back of this healthy backlog, they invested in expensive manufacturing equipment to increase capacity by 300%. Unfortunately, if the investors had visited the distributors' warehouses, they would have seen what was really happening. They were swimming in the product because consumer demand was much slower than the rate at which product was being received by the distributor. The company executives were very confident that demand would eventually pick up, but as you might guess, it did not. What they hadn't told the investors was that the customer orders were not binding so they were continuously pushed out and ultimately canceled. At that point, not only did the *additional* capacity sit idle but much of the existing capacity was not required either. The contract manufacturers who had also been lured into this shell game had hired large numbers of workers to meet the expected upsurge in demand. When it didn't materialize, major layoffs were announced, and it all turned into a fiasco. Bottom line: examine your culture of measurement and make sure you are not creating a climate of fear around it.

Given the Challenges, Is It Worth It?

It absolutely is! Grace Hopper (computing pioneer) said it best, "One accurate measurement is worth a thousand expert opinions." In the absence of good measurement, it is human nature to pay attention to the unusual or the annoying. In other words, the squeaky wheel gets the grease. Measurement instigates informed action, which provides the opportunity for people to engage in the right behavior at the right time. As management guru Peter Drucker famously said, "If you can't measure it, you can't manage it." Good metrics in your company cut through the layers of vagueness and get right to the point. Good leaders understand that measurement is important in influencing outcomes.

Now that we have established that most measurement systems are broken, despite their importance, it is time to learn how to transform these systems.

What Does "Good" Look Like?

Team members and managers are asking questions, engaging in dialogue, interacting cross-functionally, measuring value and effectiveness proactively, and discussing what they're learning through measurement. When a performance deficiency is identified, the data triggers problem-solving—not a search for who's guilty. Instead, they want to know why and what is being done to fix it. They know how to set stretch targets and then work with their teams to hit those targets.

Inevitably, what I find in organizations that are using metrics effectively is that the culture has encouraged and put a premium on dialogue. Dialogue is simply a mutual search for shared meaning or understanding. Sadly, most organizations suppress it. Bossidy and Charan, in their book *Execution*, describe dialogue as "the core of culture and the basic unit of work. Knowledge organizations are little more than the sum total of their conversations." Dialogue thrives on openness, candor, and inviting multiple viewpoints. For example, dialogue encourages conversations that start like this:

➤ **"Let's look at the measures and see how we're doing."**

➤ **"What does this data tell us about (customer satisfaction, profitability, quality)?"**

➤ **"Let's discuss why we are starting to see some improvement in this area, but not there."**

Dialogue is about encouraging frequent interactions and positive discussions about performance measurement in staff and management meetings.

Interpretation

When it comes to using metrics successfully, a key factor is not only what you measure, but how you interpret the data. For example, how often have you worked in an organization that's overly reactive to small fluctuations in a metric? If the measurement slips into the "red" for one month, the leaders overreact and pressure everyone to try harder. This leads to a lot of activity that is more busywork than value-adding. If the measurement improves in the next month your team is lauded by leadership. However, you and your team are scratching your heads because, from your vantage point, nothing has changed, which surely means that it could dip into the "red" again next month.

There will always be peaks and valleys in metrics, so you should watch for trends. Remember: *two data points don't make a trend*. A graph or a chart is a very effective way of making sense of data and metrics. It will allow you to see trends and fluctuations over time, which is where you want to focus your attention, rather than on what the performance is today. When you learn to discern a significant variation rather than reacting to routine variation, you will free up time to respond when it's appropriate and improve when it's truly necessary. Otherwise, you could find yourself reacting to a lot of noise.

Action

Measurement without action is a complete waste of time. Just as how you interpret the data is key to the success of your metrics, so is action. Ask yourself, "How long have we been measuring this?" and "What successful actions have we taken to arrive at these results?"

I have told more than one client that if they haven't acted since the last time metrics were published, it would be better to do so instead of publishing the metrics again. Unfortunately, it often takes so much time to collect the data that there is no time to perform any analysis. In other words, the ratio of analytical to administrative time is much too low. As a result, the meetings to review the metrics are more focused on what happened rather than why it happened, and what we can do about it. Ideally, if you do your analysis of the data before the meeting you can spend the meeting time figuring out the *why* of the data and not the *what*. Don't waste time in meetings on a report of the numbers. Management has already seen the numbers and doesn't need or want a rehash of the data; they want to go beyond it.

Technology

As former Marshall Industries CEO Robert Rodin said, "You can't expect technology to fix the flaws in your system. If you automate a broken process, you get an automated broken process."[1] Many organizations have impressive scorecards, dashboards, and mind-boggling analytics that provide them with little or no insight. The central problem is that organizations adopt instant, off-the-shelf scorecards zealously, which are devoid of any real value, especially once the initial glow has worn off and the consultants are gone. From my experience, most scorecard and dashboard projects have failed to provide any positive business results for the organizations adopting them.

Technology has the potential to reduce manual data handling and reduce human intervention It can prepare information so it's ready for the interpretive activity that people can do best. All too often, people scramble to put the data together from multiple sources and have no time to analyze the results. Therefore, a case can clearly be made for adding technology to make the data collection process more efficient. But tech solutions aren't going to work unless the social and organizational enablers are in place. Similarly, it's imperative that you measure your data accuracy before embarking upon an expensive technology project. IBM discovered that data quality problems cost U.S. businesses about $1.5 trillion per year—that's a hefty price tag. Much more emphasis needs to be placed on *data quality*—integrity, accuracy, ownership, and accessibility.

Furthermore, the greater the complexity of the project, the greater the possibility of failure. My advice is to start with a simpler system of metrics. If you acquire a modest version of what the system might someday evolve into, you will have a better chance of mastering it in the early stages, then evolving into something more complex as you grow. I have seen organizations that want to take the "big bang" approach. They put together a holistic set of metrics and roll them out simultaneously. This is a practice that I strongly advise against. Even one metric can take time for the organization to internalize and accept. It is important to gain alignment on many metric elements including the calculation, scope,

---

1   *Free, Perfect, and Now: Connecting to the Three Insatiable Customer Demands, a CEO's True Story*, Rodin, Robert, Free Press; Revised ed. edition (January 15, 2000).

exclusions, targets, etc. I suggest that you should start with no more than three metrics. Once you are comfortable that they are adding value, you should slowly add more to the scorecard.

In summary, your performance management system is critical to the successful management of your supply chain. However, as you have learned in this chapter, it is much more than simply selecting metrics and publishing them. There is lots to consider, but the rewards are there, if you make them a "force for good."

Mine the Gaps

Chapter 3

Phase 2:
Mine the Gaps,
Steps 1 and 2

"We are all capable of change and growth; we just need to know where to begin."

–Blaine Lee Pardoe

Step 1 – Gap Discovery

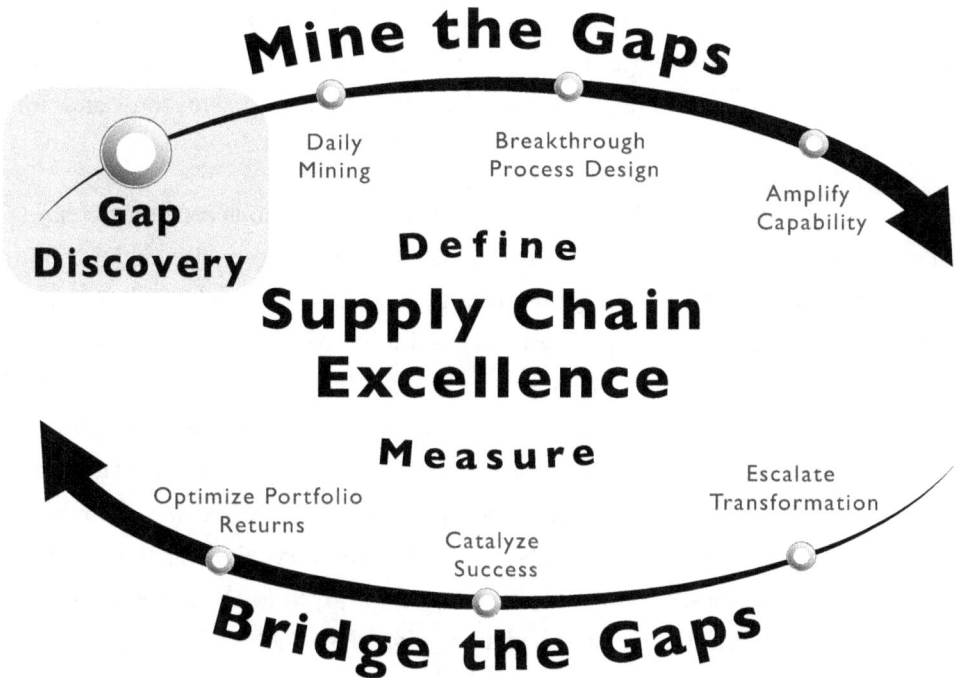

If you were walking through a manufacturing plant and noticed oil on the floor next to a machine, you would most likely think that cleaning up the oil was the right thing to do. On the surface, you would be correct, but if you dug deeper, you would realize that you only dealt with a symptom; the oil will likely come back. Now, what if I told you that the more effective action to prevent a recurrence of the problem would be to change management policy so that buyers were not just evaluated based upon PO cost? You'd probably scratch your head and wonder how I came to that conclusion. I hope at the end of this chapter, you will get it.

Gap Discovery is focused on root cause analysis, which helps us develop a deeper understanding of the problem—in this case, a leaky machine. You will learn how to utilize data to ensure that the projects you select will actually address the problem you want solved, and not a different one. In addition, you will learn to identify the few critical issues that will move the needle when solved instead of wasting time on trivial issues.

When you take the time to identify the root causes of your company's problems, you can use this knowledge to pinpoint which part of your many business processes is broken. The right process will prevent those problems from recurring. Unfortunately, most managers react impulsively and focus on symptoms and not root causes.

Ask yourself how you, as a leader, react when things don't go according to plan. In my experience, the first response is typically to point fingers elsewhere. This doesn't fix anything. Taking ibuprofen may help to soothe a headache but if the headache is caused by something serious, continuing to take painkillers rather than finding out the underlying cause isn't a very effective strategy. I once worked for a pharmaceutical company that would struggle at times to ship products on time due to sales forecasts that were invariably lower than actual shipments. This would often create product shortages and upset customers. What was the reason for this dysfunctional practice? It was because the forecasts given to the supply chain group were the same conservative projections given to Wall Street. In "supply chain speak," the forecasts had a negative bias (aka "sandbagging") . Once the real issue was identified, it was a relatively easy fix—create another forecast that was less pessimistic and more realistic than the one given to The Street. This was a company full of brilliant scientists, but unfortunately for their patients, they had not always been able to ship medications because they hadn't addressed this issue.

Once root cause analysis has been performed, your organization will know which actions and projects will have the largest impact. Compare this to how projects are usually selected in your company. In my experience, projects are rarely selected based on solving a root problem. Over my career, I've noticed a huge bias towards initiatives that simply appear "sexy." This is especially true in relation to overhyped tech, such as AI, control towers, etc. At one life science organization, they were not satisfied with their supply chain planning performance, so they decided that they needed a state-of-the-art supply chain planning solution. They had spent the past few years implementing an older system but determined that the answer to their problems lay in better technology. They ignored the fact that critical data required for accurate supply chain planning was of very low quality, and that there was inconsistency in operations. For example, the time for the quality group to approve batches could range from **90 days to 300 days**. I can assure you that the best planning technology on the planet could not overcome that level of inconsistency! In addition, bills of material (BOM) had some serious inaccuracies. However, it was difficult to quantify because this was a highly political environment, and the manufacturing department resisted publishing BOM accur acy data. They felt it would make them look bad. Worse still, departments responsible for inventory transactions, including QA and internal and external manufacturing had other priorities, so transactions were often late or inaccurate or both. As we all know, garbage inputs create garbage outputs, meaning that planners would consistently act on inaccurate Material Requirements Planning (MRP) messages.

Despite all this evidence to the contrary, it was the technology that this organization decided to change. It was quite clear that this was not going to end well. Indeed, once the selected software vendor did their due diligence, they declined to take on this doomed project. They informed the company that their data quality and operational consistency were much too low for their solution to be able to help them. The lesson here is clear: don't be seduced into thinking that a new, sophisticated technology is the first step to addressing organizational issues. To get the greatest impact, put your initial efforts into root cause analysis. Once the analysis is complete, you will be able to identify the changes necessary.

This will improve the effectiveness of your business process. Only then is it time to focus on automating the process with technology.

Once you have defined your strategic objective and metrics, it is time to look for the "gaps" that are preventing your organization from achieving your objective. Where do we find these gaps? The answer is that you will find the gaps in the "defect data." In a manufacturing environment, the defects are the products that do not meet specifications. In supply chains, however, the defects are in the form of late orders, inaccurate inventory, cost variances etc.

In these cases, defects are created by broken supply chain processes. In both cases, you'll very likely find that there are one or two gaps in your process causing most of the problems. Your goal then is to locate those specific defects that are most pertinent to the problems you're facing.

So, how do you determine which defect data is the most important? The answer depends on your strategic objective. For instance, let's say your strategic objective is to improve customer service. A good place to start would be to measure on time delivery. So you choose this as your metric for your objective. In this case, the "defect data" would be late deliveries.

Below is a list of potential improvement objectives in any supply chain:

Improvement Objective	Metric	"Defect" data:
Customer service	On-time delivery	Late deliveries
Cash flow	Inventory turns	Item excess inventory
Purchasing costs	Purchase Price Variance	PPV per PO
Logistics costs	Logistics cost as % of revenue	Shipments with cost variances
Manufacturing costs	Work order variances (material/labor)	Work orders with variances
Compliance	Number of audit observations	Audit reports
Inventory compliance	Inventory record accuracy	Cycle count errors
Supplier compliance	On-time receipt	Late receipts
Safety	Number of recordable injuries or near misses	Accident reports
Inventory scrap	Scrap$	Scrap reports

As you can see, this approach can be used for any number of strategic objectives for the supply chain. Using the table above, let's suppose that an organization's objective is to improve cash flow. On the second line, if we move to the right, we see that inventory turns—how much inventory we have relative to demand—would be the best metric to focus on. Now we need to find the "defect data." In this case, the "defect data" would be excess item inventory, or the items that have the most excess inventory relative to the design maximum (safety stock + order quantity). Luckily, this data should be readily accessible in your Enterprise Resource Planning (ERP) system! In fact, if you glance over the third column of the chart, you'll notice that most of this data should be in your ERP system. All you need to do is begin mining it.

For most of the objectives on this chart, I've achieved great results by focusing on the "defect data." For one client, the objective was improved customer service. We improved on-time delivery from below 80% to 95% in less than four months, simply by monitoring late orders on a daily basis for a few weeks in a cross-functional team environment. This approach had much more alignment and harmony than if each department was investigating these issues in silos.

Without attention to the actual gaps, the solutions to achieve a strategic objective will be interpreted differently. For example, say that a given organization's key supply chain objective was maintaining product availability. Naturally, projects that impact product availability will have the highest priority. Each department will argue that their particular project holds the highest priority to maintaining product availability. Purchasing might argue that a new MRP software is necessary to achieve the organization's objective because it will improve the planning of raw materials to avoid production line-down events. Logistics might argue that a new warehouse is required to increase the space for safety stocks. Quality could say that a new laboratory information management system is needed to speed up the release of products. Manufacturing may assert that some new, expensive piece of equipment is essential to overcoming a bottleneck. The list goes on and on and on.

Each project, when looked at in isolation, could very well be justified. Certainly, a viable business case that demonstrates a clear Return on Investment (ROI) could be drafted for each one. Each department could argue they have taken a data-driven approach, which sounds good, right? The problem is that they are not looking at the right data. Yes, they identified the problem they were facing—maintaining product availability—but they didn't use defect data to understand what was actually causing the product to be unavailable. When the root cause is discovered, the organization may realize that none of these expensive projects would have had a significant impact. Instead, they would likely find a much less expensive solution—something much different than what people would have predicted.

For example, at one organization there was an increase in material shortages on the production floor. At first, as expected, impulsive fingers were pointed and the material planning group was blamed. But when they began to dig deeper, they discovered that the materials were arriving, but were, strangely enough, stuck on the receiving dock. Even stranger was the explanation. Upon further inspection, it was discovered that the materials were failing incoming inspection. Not because the material was defective, mind you, but because the supplier had recently changed their name. Their new name wasn't on the receiving specification and so the QA department wasn't allowed to release the materials! The person responsible for changing these specifications had been backlogged and by the time they were told to change priorities, it was too late.

There's very little chance that management would have guessed this as being the source of the issue from the get-go. This is why it's important not to guess, predict, or act impulsively. Mining the gaps for "defect data" is the important first step toward resolving your company's issues effectively as it can pinpoint causes no one could anticipate. Better still, the beauty of the *Mine the Gaps* framework is that it can be applied to almost any supply chain issue.

ANALYSIS

You've avoided the impulsivity to point fingers, you've rejected the seduction of fancy tech, you've determined your company's new objective, and you've mined the gaps for "defect data." Now, what do you do with it? Recall that we're getting to the underlying root cause buried in the "defect data." If you want to discover the treasure in your "defect data," you need to interrogate it until it spills the beans. Here are three useful techniques to help you drill down toward those critical few root causes:

- ➤ **3 Levels of Fix:** A concept developed by Peter Scholtes. It showcases the benefits of moving beyond "fire fighting" to "fire prevention." This ensures that problems caused by the same root causes will not occur again.

- ➤ **Pareto Principle:** Only a few critical root causes are responsible for a majority of your problems.

- ➤ **5 Whys:** Peel back the layers of an onion until you get to the core. The crux of this technique is to keep asking why something happened until you reach the root cause.

3 LEVELS OF FIX

Peter Scholtes, who developed this concept, noticed that most organizations tended to focus on putting out the fire but would typically not find the time to prevent that same fire from recurring. Finding the time to fight fires but not to prevent them is not a great approach!

A Level 1 Fix is simply putting out the fire with no attention given to prevention. It is a symptomatic treatment, which is not an effective method of problem-solving. For those of you that have played "whack-a-mole" at the fair, you'll know how this feels. You whack the mole as it pokes up its head, only for it to pop up somewhere else.

A Level 2 Fix asks which process allowed the problem to occur. We look at the process as a whole and how it has failed rather than blaming one person or department, making it a much more effective approach. In fact, research by quality guru, Dr. Joseph Juran, revealed that over 90% of mistakes are the result of poor process design, not individual errors.

A Level 3 Fix, is by far the most effective approach. This is when you investigate how the faulty process was allowed to operate in the first place. If one faulty process slipped through the cracks, there will be more. Therefore, *Level 3 Fixes* offer the most leverage in improving supply chain performance.

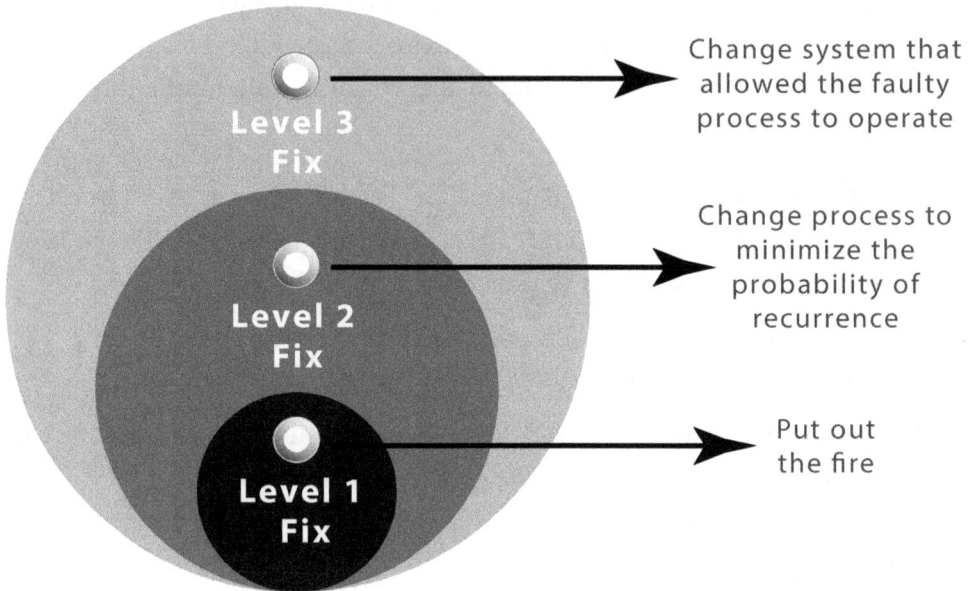

Level 3 Fix → Change system that allowed the faulty process to operate

Level 2 Fix → Change process to minimize the probability of recurrence

Level 1 Fix → Put out the fire

I'll run through a quick example that I experienced with a client. Their supply chain was primarily focused on drop shipping containers from the contract manufacturer in Asia to their U.S.-based distributors. In the period of a few weeks, there had been two instances in which the same order had inadvertently been delivered twice to the same location. This was not only embarrassing for the company, but it was a waste of resources and caused confusion for their customer. It needed to be addressed.

The *Level 1 Fix* was to send out a carrier, pick up the duplicate order, and apologize to the customer. Clearly these countermeasures would not guarantee that the same issue wouldn't happen again. Since it had happened two times in quick succession, my bet would be that it would happen again, and sooner rather than later. Senior management's answer was to reprimand the logistics coordinator for making these mistakes. However, I persuaded them to focus on the business process. It is too easy to point fingers. Unless you have a better understanding of what caused the errors, it is very likely that just blaming the person will not be a winning strategy.

After some investigation, we discovered that the logistics department received emails with the Proof of Delivery (POD) to confirm the arrival of customer orders. Unfortunately, the logistics coordinator had missed two of these emails. Therefore, it was never recorded as being delivered, prompting logistics to deliver the order again. In this case, it became apparent that the issue lay in the "Shipment Tracking" process—it was too error-prone. We immediately instructed the carrier to provide daily status reports of all in-bound shipments (*Level 2 Fix*). Now the logistics coordinator didn't have to rely upon a single email to verify the shipment's arrival. To determine whether a mistake is process-related ask, "If someone else was in that position would the same error occur?" Obviously, in this case, there is too much riding on the logistics coordinator catching every email. The process should not be designed so that only a superhero could make it work all the time. In fact, sound process design requires that a lower performer could successfully complete each step.

To drill down further, we asked how the logistics coordinator missed these two emails when he had not missed any previously? He explained that the Sales Operations Coordinator (SOC) was recently allowed to take a month-long vacation with no backup plans. This caused the Logistics Coordinator to become overwhelmed with an avalanche of emails from the sales team. In this case, the *Level 3 Fix* was to restructure the policy on vacation approval and communication, by requiring stakeholder approvals before an extended vacation is accepted. It is typical that a *Level 3 Fix* calls for a change to a management policy. As mentioned earlier, *Level 3 Fixes* also tend to have a much broader impact than on the initial case. Since difficulty covering for extended vacations is not just related to logistics, this new policy had a positive impact on many areas of the business.

THE PARETO PRINCIPLE

Back in 1906, Italian economist Vilfredo Pareto noticed that about 80% of Italy's land was owned by 20% of the population. Soon enough, it was discovered that this principle—also known as the 80/20 rule—applied to many different situations in many different disciplines, including business. And it was Joseph Juran, quality guru, who first suggested that this same principle could also apply to quality management. For example, in the context of customer service, 80% of complaints come from 20% of your customer base. In the context of profits, 80% of revenue comes from 20% of your products. And in the context of improving your supply chain, 80% of the problems are caused by 20% of the root causes.

This is more important than you might think. When you first engage in gathering "defect data," you'll find numerous root causes that you may want to address. But the Pareto Principle tells us that we should focus resources on the "critical few" root causes. See the example of a Pareto chart below for excess inventory by item. As you can see the top four causes account for about 80% of the excess inventory. The chart tells us quite clearly not to worry about the other 14 causes. How many times in your career do you think you have participated in projects that are solely focused on one of the "trivial many" causes?

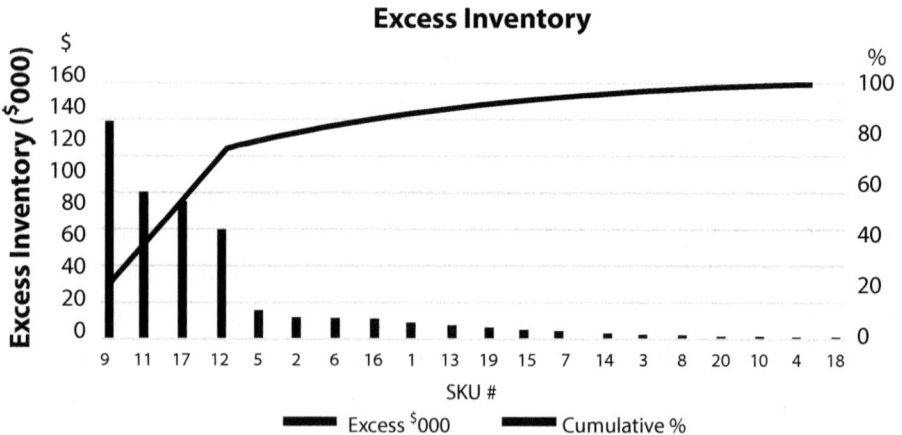

Excess Inventory

Mine the Gaps

Let's walk through an example. One client had a strategic objective to reduce logistics costs. In this case, they collected data from their ERP system on excess freight costs, i.e., shipments where the quoted cost was much lower than the actual cost. In this case, excess freight costs were their "defect data." Then they tabulated the data to find which shipments had the largest cost variance and assigned a code based on what caused each variance. As expected, 20% of the causes resulted in 80% of the excess freight costs. In this example, the two critical root causes were *port delays* and *customer delays*.

Fortunately, the client had significant control over these two issues. First, the port delays were mostly centered around the L.A. Port, so they spoke with the freight forwarder about using other west coast ports, such as Oakland.

Secondly, *customer delays* happened with drop shipments from the manufacturer in Asia to the U.S. distributor. The distributor (customer) frequently requested a delayed delivery date after the shipment had set sail from Asia. Then the client was forced to store the shipment in a third-party warehouse, incurring both storage and demurrage costs. We changed practice so that the customer was contacted before the shipment left the factory in Asia. This simple change made it far less likely that the customer would request a delayed delivery date once the shipment was in transit.

I'm quite certain that if we had asked a supply chain software vendor to solve the problem, they would have made a strong case for a state-of-the-art transportation management system. This would have been an unnecessarily expensive solution, and would have taken months to implement, whereas the chosen fix required no investment and could be implemented immediately.

As expected, the results were immediate and impressive and within several weeks, the company had reduced its logistics cost variances by 80%.

5 WHYS

The *5 Whys* technique is one of the easiest tools to understand, but that does not diminish its power. It is like when small children keep asking the question "why." For those of you who have kids, I'm sure you recognize that (sometimes) frustrating question. "Why? Why? Why?" That's your child trying to get to the root cause. And that's what you need to do.

We'll now return to the oil spill example that I introduced at the start of the chapter. The first question was, *"Why is this puddle on the floor and what can we do about it?"*

Level of Problem	Corresponding level of countermeasure
There is a puddle of oil on the shop floor	Clean up the oil
Because the machine is leaking oil	Fix the machine
Because the gasket has deteriorated	Replace the gasket
Because we bought gaskets made of inferior material	Change gasket specifications
Because we got a good deal (price) on those gaskets	Change purchasing policies
Because the buyer gets evaluated on cost savings	**Change the evaluation policy for buyers**

The answer? Because the machine is leaking. *Why?* The gasket has deteriorated. *Why?* We purchased gaskets made from inferior material. *Why?* We wanted to purchase gaskets at a low price. *Why?* Because the buyer is evaluated on cost savings.

Boom! After *5 Whys* we have the root cause: there's oil on the floor because management rewards purchasing for reduced costs. Referring to the table above, we can see that the most impactful fix to this root cause is to change the evaluation policy for the buyers. The other countermeasures may help, but unless the root cause is addressed, management will always be pressured to purchase low-cost, low-quality items. Again, we see that it is management policies that have the most impact on supply chain performance.

From what we have covered, we can see that root cause analysis leverages historical data that is frequently at our fingertips. This data is powerful, because the past tends to repeat itself, so it frequently predicts future events. However, we can't rely on historical data alone. It is necessary, but not sufficient. In the next section, we'll look at how to leverage *current supply chain data* to help us understand chronic issues afflicting our supply chains.

Step 2 – Daily Mining

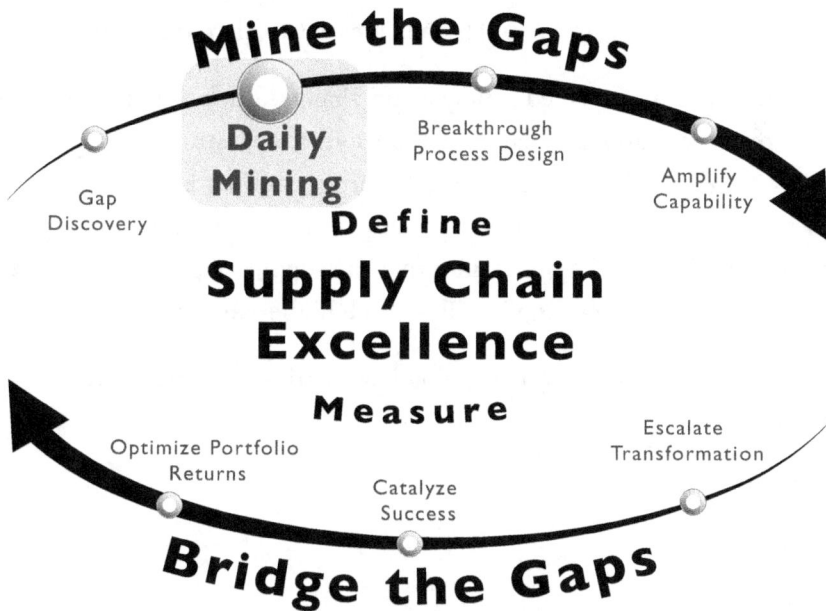

The COVID-19 pandemic has reminded us that supply chains are inherently dynamic. Unplanned events occur all the time, making it imperative to regularly review the daily supply chain status. All too often, I visit clients that rarely or never meet as an operational group. At one organization, cross-functional meetings to discuss these daily details were very infrequent. They tried to remain in tune to daily disruptions via email. When a disruption occurs, there is rarely only one possible response, and the best option is not always clear until each function involved has had their say. These daily meetings ensure that everyone is rowing in the same direction. Once the client started to meet several times per week, internal coordination became much better. On-time delivery improved from less than 50% to more than 90% within three months. Whenever an order was late, the reason for the delay was collectively agreed upon. In the absence of these meetings, each group would have a different understanding of the delay. As a result, there was minimal organizational learning to better prepare the company for the next disruption. When a team looks at the same problem together, it is amazing how much easier it is to reach consensus about the root cause and the appropriate course of action. Just like historical data, after a short period, chronic issues will become clear, and it will be much easier to align on the path forward.

Frequent review of unexpected supply chain changes, such as non-forecasted customer orders or supplier delays, buys precious time to mitigate the risk created by the disruption. For example, if a large customer is lost, it could become necessary to reschedule or cancel a supplier purchase order. The longer this action is not taken, the higher the probability that the supplier will not accept the request, or the cost for granting it will become higher and higher.

Daily reviews should begin by displaying key metrics associated with the operation.

TOPICS SHOULD INCLUDE:

- ➤ **Safety**
- ➤ **Quality**
- ➤ **Delivery**
- ➤ **Inventory**
- ➤ **Productivity**

The metrics are visually displayed, so that the current status of the area is obvious immediately. This contrasts with how many organizations operate. In these organizations, reports are prepared and distributed to senior management, who are charged with interpreting the data to develop the appropriate actions. This approach will always create misinterpretations, leading to bad decisions and discord as employees shake their heads in wonderment at how out of touch their management team is.

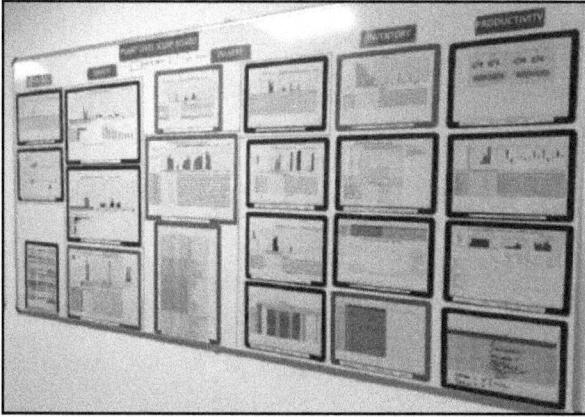

The overall purpose of these meetings should be open and honest discussion. Without that, the team will not reach a full understanding of the situation. It is also important to remember that the business process is the focus so that gradually, "process muscle" is built. This is also a great opportunity for employees to become better problem solvers. A senior leader who is skilled in problem solving and who works with the team each day will be much more effective in teaching employees than formal training.

Mine the Gaps

Chapter 4

Phase 2:
Mine the Gaps,
Step 3

*"If you can't describe what you are doing as a process,
you don't know what you're doing."*

–W. Edwards Deming

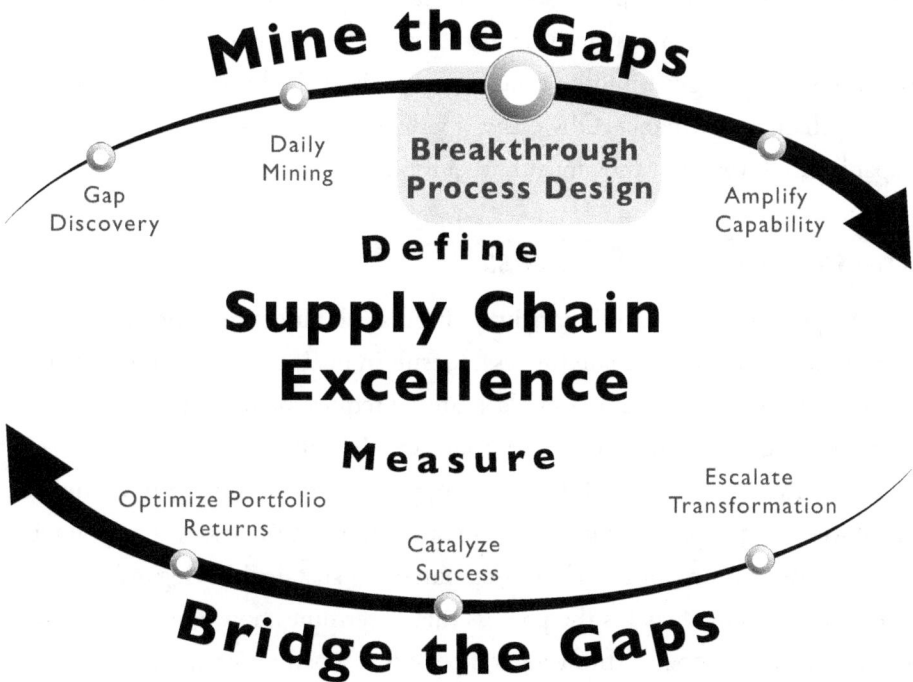

Mine the Gaps

Gap Discovery

Daily Mining

Breakthrough Process Design

Amplify Capability

D e f i n e
Supply Chain Excellence
M e a s u r e

Optimize Portfolio Returns

Catalyze Success

Escalate Transformation

Bridge the Gaps

How often have you worked at an organization that meets its goals most quarters by brute force with minimal finesse? The team becomes adrenaline junkies as they consistently perform miraculous feats and are rewarded by their bosses each time. In many organizations this becomes the norm. The results are achieved via different chaotic means, each time.

In this chapter, you'll learn about a better way to function—one where work is performed consistently each time. You'll learn the principles related to how work gets done, with many examples of each principle related to life science supply chains.

Just as an expert mechanic can pull apart an engine and redesign it to transform a car's performance, we can redesign business processes to dramatically improve your supply chain performance. However, whether the redesign efforts have achieved their purpose cannot be decided by the engineers. Since the customer is the one that decides whether to procure a product or service, only they get to decide if the business processes are indeed creating valuable outputs. In this chapter, you will learn how to hear the voice of the customer (VOC) and design processes accordingly. Building process muscle is at the heart of how to improve supply chain performance. Obviously, it will always require enthusiastic and capable employees, but they must have a robust process to guide them.

The Importance of Process

Simply put, processes turn inputs into outputs. Manufacturing processes result in products, and supply chain processes result in business deliverables, such as purchase orders, bills of materials, material requirements planning (MRP) messages, etc. Sometimes process outputs are high quality, low cost and on-time; at other times, as we all know, the opposite is true. You can have the best employees on the planet, but if they are operating bad processes then you will not achieve your organization's desired outcomes sustainably. Regardless of the talents of an individual, it's the process that determines how a business performs. As the old saying goes, "Throw a good person at a bad process, the process will always prevail."

The consulting company, Gartner, says that business process management (BPM) is "a management discipline that treats processes as assets that directly contribute to enterprise performance outcomes [in other words, results] by driving operational excellence." Taken from another perspective, a bad process directly contributes to bad results. For instance, poor supply chain planning processes could lead to excess inventory, bad customer service, stockouts, or scrap. Inadequate sourcing processes can create low quality materials, late deliveries, or high material costs. In addition, poor logistics processes can result in product recalls, shipping errors, shipping damages, high transportation costs, line-down events… the list of problems goes on and on and on. And all are problems that could be avoided with an effective process design and execution.

And yet, strangely enough, business executives have a difficult time seeing the value of process improvement and operational innovation. Executives tend to have their own ideas on how to improve the company, based on their own experience rather than data. It's like that old parable of the six blind men describing an elephant—one focuses on technology, another on human resource issues, a third on organizational structure, etc. An actual analysis into data-driven process development doesn't interest them. I've spoken with many managers from innumerable industries and companies who all tell a similar story. When they've tried to inform their senior executives about the importance of operational innovation, the senior execs quickly shut them down. As one manager said, "In our company, operations are not glamorous. Deals are."

Making acquisitions, planning mergers, and buying and selling divisions will get the company's name and the CEO's picture in business magazines. Redesigning procurement or transforming product development will not, even though it's these very factors which would improve the company's performance. It's obvious that a shift in perspective needs to occur and that process improvement should be taken seriously.

In this chapter, I'll give you the basic rundown on how to analyze and improve your current process so your supply chain operates smoothly, and you can get a good night's sleep. I like to call it "building process muscle," as each process improvement is like a workout: creating an increasingly healthy body or organization.

Process Redesign Steps

Throughout my career, whenever I have been asked to improve supply chain performance, my starting point has often been to evaluate business processes. In many cases, there was no process to evaluate so it needed to be designed from scratch.

Normally, the first step is to form a cross-functional team of those involved in the process, and then take the following steps:

1. **Define the problem or objective**

2. **Develop a SIPOC**

3. **Map out the current state**

4. **Redesign:**

    a. **Identify pain points and opportunities**

    b. **Apply process redesign principles and develop future state**

1. DEFINE THE PROBLEM OR OBJECTIVE

As the adage goes... "A problem well-defined is half solved." Never were truer words spoken. It seems obvious that before you can fix a problem, you need to know what it is. From my experience, it is typical for lots of energy to be expended solving a problem, only to find out that the problem wasn't properly understood and so the solution was off the mark. As you might expect, this just leads to rework, delays and frustration. To properly define a problem (or objective), it should be clear and concise. For example, to say that "overtime has increased by 30%" is not clear enough for several reasons:

➤ Time period: We don't know by when the problem must be solved, or over what period the overtime increased.

➤ Scope: Is the overtime in one department, one site or all sites?

➤ Unit of measure: Is it the cost per hour of overtime that has increased by 30%, the number of labor hours or a combination of both?

> Business Impact: if you want to sell this project to senior management, they will want to know what impact it will have on the bottom line.

2. DEVELOP A **SIPOC**

Before you can set about making your process better, you should start with a SIPOC. No, this is not an alien from outer space! A SIPOC answers the following questions related to the business processes under examination:

> Who are the **S**uppliers of the inputs?

> What are the **I**nputs to the process?

> What are the key steps of the **P**rocess?

> What are the process **O**utputs?

> Who are the **C**ustomers of the outputs?

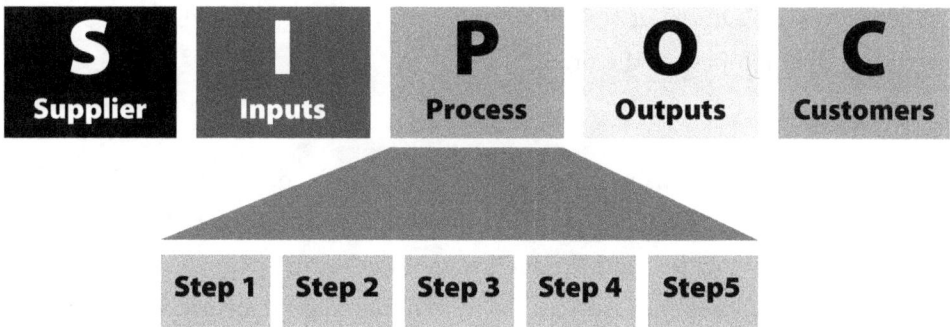

OUTPUTS

A SIPOC is a high-level view of the process you're implementing or redesigning. Think about your daily job. Do you know which business processes are required to make your job successful? Probably not, because people don't normally think this way. However, if you ask someone what outputs they are responsible for, you likely get a more definite response. For example, what outputs are the purchasing department responsible for? In other words, if the purchasing department ceased to exist, what would stop happening? Purchase orders would not be placed, suppliers would not be qualified and selected for new materials, supplier quality issues would not be resolved, item and vendor master files would not be maintained, and so on.

Now that you have defined the outputs, so what? As I discussed earlier, outputs are generated by business processes. In other words, now that you know the outputs, you can work backwards to define the business process. In the case of the purchasing department, the following connection between outputs and business processes can be made:

1. Place purchase orders—PO process

2. Qualify and select suppliers—supplier qualification and selection process

3. Resolve supplier quality issues—material review process

For example, say the purchasing department was experiencing mistakes in orders placed with suppliers. In this case, what is the output? That's right, purchase orders and the PO process should be evaluated to understand what causes the errors, and which part of the process is broken.

CUSTOMERS

Once the output and business process have been defined, you need to identify who your customer is, and what they want. The most important customers are the ones that pay for your products obviously, but many process outputs go to an internal customer. You still need to understand their needs so that it delivers exactly what they need to make them more effective and efficient. These internal processes will eventually lead to an external customer, so efficient and effective internal processes will lead to quality, inexpensive and on-time outputs. Determining the voice of the customer (VOC) helps your company understand what the customers want, and what they consider to be important. Ask your customers what their expectations are and how your company measures up to those expectations.

So how can you get a good grasp on the VOC? A common mistake is falsely assuming that you already know the needs of your customers. To discover a customer's wants, you need to hear it from the horse's mouth because only the customer knows what the customer wants. Taking the time to do this will pay dividends in the long run. Questions like these are of extreme benefit to discovering what metrics are critical to quality (CTQ) to the customer.

After this, you can then cross-reference your customers' expectations with your own targets and results. Do they match up? Do we successfully satisfy the customer's needs? Take on-time delivery, for example. How well do we deliver against our commitments?

PROCESS

The next step is to focus on the "P"—process—which involves defining a few high-level steps in the process. One key reason to do this is that it will help you define the start and end of the process, which may seem obvious, but believe me, it is not. Ask 10 team members where the process starts and where it ends, and you will likely get 11 answers. For example, earlier we referred to the Purchase Order process; where does it start and end? Does it start with obtaining a signal that a purchase order needs to be placed, when the purchase requisition is first routed for approval, or when it is entered into your ERP system? In addition, where does it end? Is it when the PO is acknowledged by the supplier, when it is delivered, when it is received, when it is quality released, or when the supplier is paid? There is not necessarily a right answer, except to say that if there is a specific problem that you'd like to fix, then narrow the process scope to only include the segment of the process relevant to the problem. However, if you have a broader objective to optimize the end-to-end business process, then you should include all steps. In this case, the end-to-end process is generally known as the Purchase to Pay process.

INPUTS/SUPPLIERS

Next it is time to focus on inputs. Each step of the process defined will require inputs and those inputs will have suppliers. In the PO case, one step could be to create and route requisition for approval. What are some of the key inputs here?

1. Approval matrix: Your company will typically have a document that defines who must approve the requisition based upon what is being purchased and the dollar value of the purchase order.

2. Routing system: Is it routed via a workstream within your ERP system, or a document approval software?

The suppliers could be:

1. Approval matrix: CFO

2. Routing system: IT

These inputs can also have quality requirements. In other words, what level of quality is required to achieve the desired results? For example, errors in the approval matrix cannot be tolerated, so its accuracy target must be 100%. Without these requirements, it is difficult to control the quality of the purchase order itself. No matter how good a chef is, if the quality of ingredients is not of a good standard, then the meal will be disappointing.

3. Map Out the Current State

The process map is the next step to process management improvement. While a SIPOC is a good way to get an overall view of your current process, a process map (see below) provides much more detail and defines each step of the process.

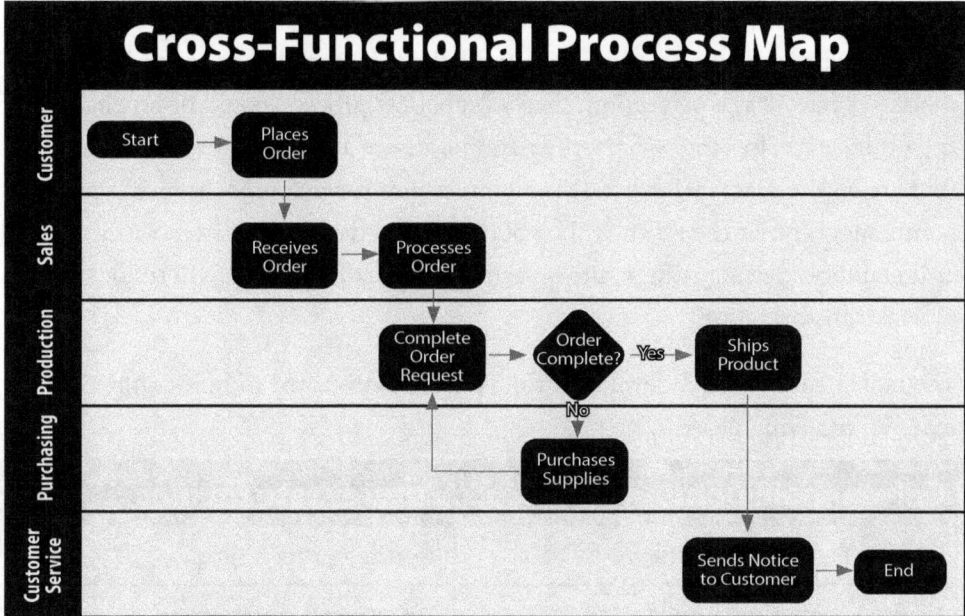

It's called a "swim lane" process map because each horizontal line is like a swimming lane. Each individual lane is representative of a different department or role, detailing their specific responsibilities for each part of the process. Each time there is a hand-off, there is a high probability that delays and miscommunications will happen.

The primary purpose of a process map is to find opportunities for improvement, otherwise you should not create one at all. The last thing you want is to put in the time and effort into mapping out these responsibilities only for it to end up being wallpaper for your company to occasionally glance at.

4. REDESIGNING YOUR PROCESS

a. *Pain points and opportunities*

First ask the team to identify "pain points" associated with the current process. In addition, ask internal or external customers of the business process what their headaches are. If possible, assign each pain point to a step in the process. Next, translate pain points to a general vision for the future state. For example, if too much paperwork is a pain point, then a "paperless process" could be an element of the future state. In other words, the pain points are an insight into general themes that are on the team's wish list. It is a more aspirational approach. Fixing pain points suggest that the result will be better than today, but not necessarily as good as it could be. Setting your sights on achieving broader themes will result in more radical transformation.

The table below is one I developed for a client that wanted to redesign their material receiving process:

Current pain points	Future state themes
Several Excel tracking files	Remove Excel files
Manual metric data collection	Automated key metrics
Several paper forms	Paperless process
Manual/email notifications	Automated notifications
Receiving delayed due to missing docs	Minimize receiving delays
Inaccurate master data	Accurate master data
Inaccurate process documentation	Accurate work instructions

Now that you have defined the current state, pain points, and opportunities, it is time to redesign the process. There are seven redesign principles that can literally transform how work gets done in your organization. If you apply these principles to each step of the process flow, you will find many potential improvement opportunities. One thing to note, however, is that you shouldn't get too hung up on which principle a specific improvement falls under. These principles are meant only to jog your memory and get you to think more holistically about how to improve the supply chain in your organization.

Ask the team to examine each step of the process and to explore whether any of the below seven process redesign principles can be applied to improve the process:

1. WHAT?

The first question is **What** steps will be included in the process. The only steps in your process flow that need to remain are those that add value. Any other steps should be eliminated or minimized if possible. But how, you may be asking, do we determine which steps add value? Some of you may already know the answer... Yes, the customer! The customer is who determines value. I can't stress this enough, but do not assume that you already know your customer's needs. Like any relationship, you may have been hyperattentive to the needs of your customer... in the beginning. After a while, it's easy to take your partner (in this case, your customer) for granted and ignore their needs.

For example, I knew of a company who was very proud of their on-time delivery performance to their customers. Sounds good, right? Well, eventually the customer pointed out that the company's lead times from the order placement to the order delivery ranged from a few days to a few weeks, with little consistency. The customer explained that this varying lead time made it difficult for them to plan their inventory. They preferred a standard, consistent lead, rather than one that varied from order to order, even if they did meet their commit date.

2. WHETHER AND UNDER WHAT CIRCUMSTANCES

Obviously, eliminating an unnecessary step from the process is ideal, but your next best option is to decide **Whether and Under What Certain Circumstances** a step can be eliminated. Too often, organizations have the same approach no matter what. For example, you receive a bill in the mail for less than 10 cents, even though the cost of the billing process is orders of magnitude higher. Why? Because nobody thought to set a minimum invoice amount in the billing process. This is an example of where inserting a checkpoint in the process can add significant value to the organization.

Another good example are auto insurance claims. The largest type of claim is windshield breakage. Generally, when a claim is made, an adjuster is sent out to evaluate the damage, but what insurance companies eventually realized is that windshield claims almost always result in the same outcome—a new windshield. Insurance companies concluded that it would be more cost effective to replace the windshield without the adjuster seeing the damage in person.

At one medical device organization, I led an initiative with the purchasing group to redesign their supplier quality program. Previously, all suppliers were treated the same whether they supplied cardboard boxes or complex instruments. They liked to think that all their suppliers were important, but as we all know, if we plan to treat every supplier as important, then none of them will be treated as important. Why? Because there are simply not enough resources to give all their suppliers white-glove attention. We had to redesign the process so that higher risk suppliers were managed more carefully via periodic audits and regular business reviews, whereas lower risk suppliers were given far less attention.

3. WHO?

Who is doing the work is just as important as what the work is, and it's also the most common type of change. The **Who** principle really determines what skill level is required to complete a task, whether it should be lowered or increased in certain areas. For example, in many organizations, the processing of a customer order flows through multiple departments: sales, order management, credit, production planning, manufacturing, distribution, accounts receivable, and on and on the list goes. From the moment the order is received to the point the customer is billed, there is no single person responsible for the entire process. However, caseworkers can often be brought on to take this responsibility and shepherd the order from point A to point B, while also being the only point of contact for the customer. This often leads to huge improvements in lead time, accuracy, reduced cost, and customer satisfaction.

4. WHEN?

You can apply the **When** principle by moving certain steps earlier or later in the process. For instance, when purchase orders are placed with suppliers the supplier checks capacity, material availability, and then gives you a lead time. But there may be an opportunity to reserve capacity ahead of time based on a forecast. Later, the specific item can be selected closer to the need date. By conducting this step earlier, you reduce your lead time, which means that you carry less inventory and minimize supply risk.

Another application of this principle is by performing steps in parallel instead of sequentially, which typically reduces overall lead time. Let's say you're performing a changeover from one product to another on the manufacturing floor. Often, this means that fixtures and equipment need to be changed, which can take time. But this time can be reduced by analyzing which steps can be performed while the machine is running the previous product. These parallel performing steps are called "external" steps, while steps that are sequential are called "internal." The more external steps that can be performed, the quicker the changeover time and the less capacity lost.

5. WHERE?

The next question to ask is **Where** the work should be done. For instance, where should you store low-demand finished goods items—in one centralized location or in multiple locations globally? Since it is generally more difficult to forecast low-demand items, it's usually a good idea to centralize your inventory storage. Otherwise, the safety stock required to buffer against forecast error in multiple locations will be cost prohibitive.

6. How precisely?

It is possible that, upon examination, you may find that a step doesn't need to be performed as thoroughly or as **Precisely** as previously thought. The opposite can also occur, and you may find that a given step needs more precision. To give an example of the former circumstance, rough cut capacity planning (RCCP) is much less precise than detailed capacity planning. RCCP uses aggregate production plan quantities at the product family level, rather than at the specific, detailed item level. Instead of a bill of material, a bill of resource is used, which only contains critical resources and the relationship of their usage to the production volume. For example, if you worked for a bicycle manufacturer, it would be relatively easy to calculate the relationships between production volume and the amount of frame material required, whether it is aluminum, carbon, steel, or titanium. It is unnecessary to do detailed capacity planning, which includes many inputs such as work order data, routings, bills of materials, work center data, etc. that many organizations struggle to manage effectively. As a result, they end up creating very precise, but very inaccurate, capacity plans.

7. What information to use?

These days, organizations can create endless data, which can be quite overwhelming. Data is so readily available that many of us don't know which bits to ignore and which bits to savor and take seriously. For instance, many organizations calculate their safety stock levels by simply keeping x weeks' supply for all items. But demand variability may differ hugely from one item to another, meaning that historical demand data should be utilized to calculate demand variability and appropriate safety stock levels to maintain service level objectives without overstocking. I'll give you one more example. A client's material warehouse was overflowing and management had budgeted for a new $2 million warehouse. All we needed to do was walk through the warehouse and we could quickly see that the racks were not well utilized. Even though the aisles were completely congested, there was a lot of unused space. In less than two hours, we estimated that only 60% of rack space was being utilized and quickly determined there was no need for a new warehouse. In fact, our reconfiguration was so successful that we were able to remove racks from a third of the warehouse and repurpose the space. All it took was an examination of the right data to avoid a $2 million capital expenditure. See the pattern here?

Final Tips

Now that we have reviewed the seven redesign principles, I'd like to add a couple pieces of advice to make your process redesign efforts more successful:

ANALYSIS PARALYSIS

I once worked at a large pharmaceutical company that took over six months to develop their Sales and Operations Planning process. It is impossible to foresee the issues that will arise once the new process has been implemented. Therefore, spend a little time on process design, implement the new process, and then continuously solicit feedback. During each cycle of the process, you should expect to make a few improvements and, after a few months, your process will be much smoother and aligned with the needs of the stakeholders. Alternatively, if you spend the same amount of time designing the "perfect" process, it is likely that it will be over-engineered with too many steps added to please everyone and to cover all possible scenarios, both real and imagined. Once you go live, you'll realize much of the functionality is unnecessary and nobody has the bandwidth to maintain it anyway.

This method is like the agile approach to project management, where one important principle is to start with the "Minimum Viable Product" (MVP). The 80/20 rule comes into play again, meaning that 20% of product (or process) features add 80% of the value. Figure out what is most critical and necessary to get started, and work from there. Sales and Operations Planning (S&OP) implementation is a good example of this. You can listen to the consultants and design a full-blown S&OP program, but does your organization really require all the functionality? Not necessarily, especially for smaller organizations.

For example, a small biotech company asked me to implement S&OP. They had previously attempted to launch it, but it failed due to lack of interest—to the extent that sometimes nobody would show up to the meetings. I inquired why this was the case, and it was primarily because the S&OP leader would show tons and tons of slides, which he felt were necessary in an S&OP process. He failed to ask the stakeholders what they wanted to see and was then surprised when nobody showed up. In addition, there was very little interaction in the meetings; it was him talking and the others just listening. S&OP meetings are supposed to be interactive, with plenty of questions and dialogue.

I immediately recognized that the most important topic for the organization was ensuring finished goods availability once the FDA approved their first commercial product. In the beginning, that was the only item on the agenda. We received updates on forecasts, actual production, quality releases, rejected batches, and projected inventory levels. While this may seem easy enough, if you want to use planning best practices, even this takes time. For example, the commercial group provided forecasts, but they would constantly change without explanation. We worked with them to understand the key assumptions behind their forecasts, so we knew which assumptions changed when the forecast was updated. We found that the commercial group did not want to share this information, and the organization didn't seem in a hurry to pressure them to do so. We also reported on actual output and changes to the production plan. I was told that one of the senior executives within the operations organization was uncomfortable sharing this information with the commercial group, in case the numbers didn't paint a pretty picture.

This is a good test of organizational maturity and readiness for a cross-functional process like S&OP. It is not until you start the process that organizational readiness is tested. If the organization is not ready, you'll be grateful that you didn't spend months designing a process that looks great on paper but not in practice. In this case, it didn't take long to realize that unless this initiative was sponsored at the highest levels of the organization, it was doomed to failure.

➤ Be Effective, Then Efficient

Finally, I'd like to give this word of warning about process improvement. Processes are the key leverage point to create better results. Technology should support the process, but I caution heavily against automating before your process has matured. Automating an immature process will freeze your process at that level of maturity, since technology is expensive and time-consuming to implement. Once you have proceeded down the automation route, making the technology work now becomes the focus instead of improving your process. While I have never met a business process that is immediately perfect, I have experienced many times when a redesigned business process stagnates in its early stages of maturity. This is typically because technology was applied too quickly and became frozen in time even though it was not yet ready.

Instead, once a newly designed process is operational, observe it and seek feedback from the stakeholders. There will undoubtedly be gaps and room for improvement. If there are no efforts to improve it at the early stages, it will never perform to its potential, and its outputs will always be a disappointment. On the other hand, if you continuously solicit feedback and act upon it, the process will improve until it reaches a "steady state." In other words, improvement opportunities slow down from an avalanche in the beginning to a slow trickle. At that point, the process can be considered effective. It will be generating outputs of high quality, on time, and cost effectively. However, it will still involve too many manual steps, so it will be effective but inefficient. Now is the time to introduce technology and automation! Technology can enable the processes to become efficient and even more effective since manual steps are often associated with mistakes and a lack of consistency. Follow these guidelines and your supply chain performance should transform quickly and sustainably for the long term.

Mine the Gaps

Chapter 5

Phase 2:
Mine the Gaps,
Step 4

"There are far better things ahead than any we leave behind."

–C.S. Lewis

Mine the Gaps

Gap Discovery

Daily Mining

Breakthrough Process Design

Amplify Capability

Define

Supply Chain Excellence

Measure

Optimize Portfolio Returns

Catalyze Success

Escalate Transformation

Bridge the Gaps

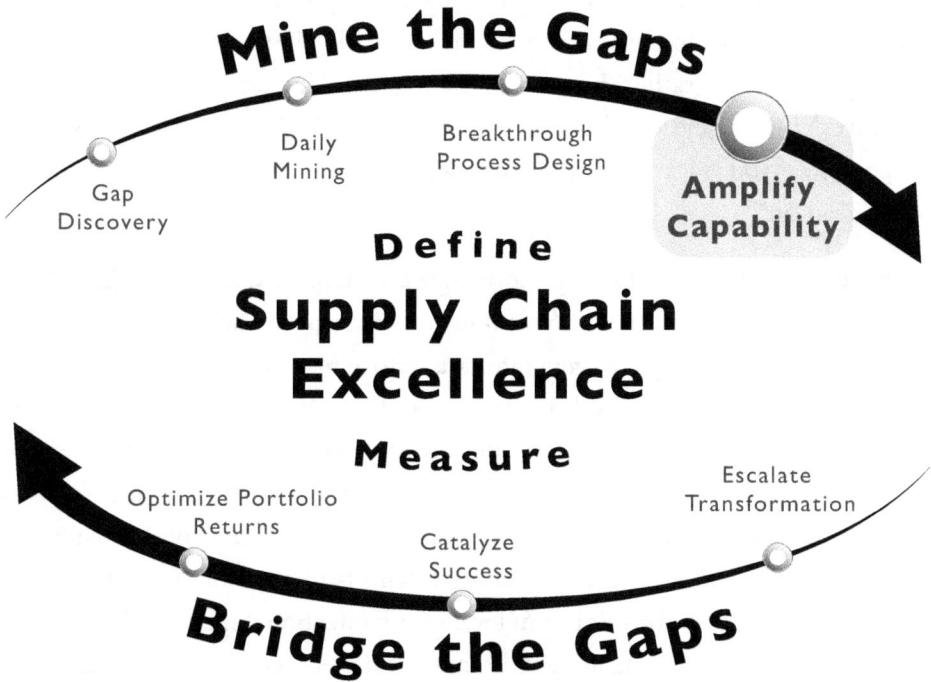

Most organizations start their journey with an underperforming supply chain and want to improve its effectiveness and efficiency. For most organizations, the biggest questions are, what does that look like and how do we get there? What if there was an assessment tool that described the key domains for advancing all aspects of your organization to the next capability level?

➤ **People**

➤ **Business Processes**

➤ **Data**

➤ **Metrics**

➤ **Technology**

➤ **Lean**

This assessment tool will enable you to uncover a more holistic set of gaps. Once the team has developed solutions to these gaps, they can then be prioritized based upon your business needs. The assessment tool will help to create a roadmap using a structured process rather than a cobbled-together, diverse set of departmental initiatives? I have developed that exact tool and methodology for just this purpose, so if you want to improve your supply chain's effectiveness and efficiency, please read on!

As discussed earlier, to achieve performance excellence requires capable and engaged **people**. However, without robust **business processes**, it will always be a struggle for good people to generate satisfactory results. Business processes require accurate **data**, but until the process itself has been defined, you don't know which data is necessary. As with any journey, we must define where we want to go, measure where we are today, as well as our progress along the route. In other words, it is important to have effective **metrics** within a robust performance management system. If your organization attempts to focus on metrics before accurate data exists and a minimum level of organizational maturity is achieved, you will waste time arguing about whether the data is accurate and which department is to blame. Instead, first focus on leveraging metrics to develop a cross-functional understanding of how the organization is performing against certain metrics and aligning efforts to improve. At this point, it is important to select and implement **technology** that will support the business processes, data management, and performance management.

Once significant progress is achieved in the previous domains, your supply chain will have standardized processes that are performing effectively. However, even the best supply chains have a significant number of wasteful practices so implementing a lean program to identify and eliminate the waste will enable continuous improvement. It is not advisable to focus too much on "leaning" out your supply chain until the previous domains have created repeatable and consistent results. In other words, first focus on effectiveness and then focus on efficiency. If you attempt to make an ineffective process more efficient, **you will merely fail more quickly!**

The 6 Stages of Capability Development:

STAGE 1 – UNDER-PERFORMING

Your supply chain results are falling short of expectations because each of the six domains are immature. It is likely that your processes are unreliable, which causes lots of expediting, firefighting and heroics. You have many metrics, but they are ill-defined with minimal ownership or accountability. Management creates an unhealthy environment due to an over-emphasis on results and meeting targets so there is lots of finger-pointing, gaming of the metrics and minimal collaboration. Data is unreliable and requires much cleansing before it is usable, which leaves little time for analysis and understanding the root cause of performance issues.

Top management and employees are generally unaware of operational excellence and supply chain best practices. They do not understand the importance of the role that sponsors play in the success of projects, so benefits are seldom realized. The ERP system is more focused on finance than supply chain and there are disparate systems of record (SOR). Planning is typically done in MS Excel, and there is minimal integration with supply chain partners. Lead times are long and variable, forecasts are inaccurate, batch sizes are large, and set up time is high. This causes low inventory turns and unsatisfactory on-time delivery.

Stage 2 – Progressing

The focus at this stage is to develop people capability, improve data accuracy and continue to develop the high-leverage processes. Executive management recognizes the need for change and effectively communicates it to employees. Employees have been included early in the change process, to facilitate buy-in instead of feeling like something is being done to them.

Supply chains require lots of data, and so it will take time to achieve the necessary level of accuracy for all data elements. However, there are a few elements that should be focused on immediately:

1. Inventory records

2. Bill of materials

3. Lead time accuracy

4. Scheduled receipt due dates (work orders/purchase orders)

Each of these elements should be at 95% before this stage is completed. One key data element left off this list is forecast accuracy. Although reduction of forecast error is a vital part of improving supply chain performance, I would not advocate focusing on it at this step. For now, we'll focus on a particular type of forecast inaccuracy: forecast bias. This is the worst type of inaccuracy because it is deliberately induced by management practices. Bias is when the forecast is consistently over or under actual demand. The other type of forecast inaccuracy is random variation, in which actual demand fluctuates above or below the forecast each month.

Since data accuracy is still an issue in Stage 2, there is little point in focusing on metrics, since you'll spend most of your time cleansing the data and arguing about its validity. However, it's important to establish robust data accuracy metrics at this stage so you know when the 95% target has been achieved. If organizational alignment can be easily achieved for inventory turns, supplier on-time delivery, manufacturing schedule adherence and on-time customer delivery, they can be introduced at this stage, otherwise it would be better to wait until Stage 3.

In terms of technology, if an ERP system has not been selected yet, supply chain requirements should be defined at this stage. If the ERP system has been implemented, it should meet 80% of the requirements. Sales and Operations Planning (S&OP) may have been initiated, but it is likely at a low level of maturity, with a short-term tactical focus. Minimal effort should be expended at this stage to increase the effectiveness of the process.

STAGE 3 – EFFECTIVE

At this stage, executive sponsorship should be very active and visible, which generates energy and engagement to build momentum around the change. The team has been taught problem solving skills, such as root cause analysis, so that issues are addressed more effectively, and a continuous improvement mindset is more prevalent. There is an executive coalition that drives cross-functional collaboration. S&OP has helped product planning, demand planning and supply planning be much better integrated. Core supply chain processes have been transitioned to the ERP system.

The critical few best practices have been identified and implemented effectively, and the benefits are now being realized. Valid data should be sufficiently available so that key metrics such as on-time customer delivery, manufacturing adherence to the plan, on time supplier delivery and inventory turns are now measured. Initial usage of business intelligence tools will support access to the data so there is more time for analysis. Finally, when metrics are discussed in management meetings, the organization embraces the results and engages in a healthy debate to decide what action is needed to improve performance.

STAGE 4 – STANDARDIZED

Now that you have an effective supply chain system, focus on institutionalizing the practices and improvements achieved so far. Policies, processes, and procedures should all be documented. The key, however, is that top management has authorized these documents, and they are driving the business.

STAGE 5 – PERFORMING

Since processes are followed and fully documented, continuous improvement and problem solving via root cause analysis is now routine. Gaps from supply chain best practices are well-defined, and variation reduction techniques are effectively utilized. At this stage, a key element is that relationships with supply chain partners are much closer, which enables further efficiencies. More advanced technology solutions can be utilized internally and to integrate with partners.

STAGE 6 – SUSTAINED EXCELLENCE

At this stage, business processes are fully integrated with key supply chain partners. All supply chain members are committed to rapid response and short lead times. Improvements in product design have simplified the supply chain with few components and a smaller supply base. Decision making is such that it yields the best financial performance for the company. Scenario planning helps to optimize plans. All these improvements have transformed performance relative to perfect orders, inventory turns, asset utilization, costs and throughput speeds.

SUPPLY CHAIN PLANNING CAPABILITY MODEL

We can look at how to use this capability model for assessment of supply chain planning. For example, we are looking at the "People" domain in the table on the next page. Which level best describes the capability of your organization? In most cases, companies have characteristics that appear in more than one level, so they select the one that best describes them. In this example, they determine that *Level 2* best describes their capability. The next step is to review the characteristics of the levels immediately above and below the current state, in this case, *Levels 1* and *3*, and highlight the characteristics that must still be bridged.

| Domain | People | Current |
Level	Description	Level
1	Employees and top management have minimal understanding of, or experience with, supply chain planning processes or operational excellence. General organizational lack of awareness of the need for change. Key information such as company financials is not shared with employees.	
2	Awareness of the need for change is communicated by top management, including sharing of key information such as market conditions and competitive threats to build the "burning platform." Top management have received executive education and explicitly communicated their support. Employees have been engaged early in the process.	**X**
3	Basic concepts of supply chain planning, how to use the ERP system and operational excellence principles are understood. Super users have been identified for more advanced training e.g., green/black belt, APICS. Executive sponsorship is active and visible. Sponsorship coalition has been formed. Energy and engagement around the change has produced momentum. Short terms wins are sought and celebrated.	
4	Formal change management assessment and training plan, including supervisor change/resistance management training. Supervisors have received training on the coaching role. Clear feedback channels have been created to identify gaps in process or technology. Super users have been trained and serve as mentors and coaches.	
5	Employees are routinely demonstrating their ability to implement changes. Hands-on demos and coaching is routinely available. Appropriate skills are developed or hired to perform analysis and communicate results to make decisions.	
6	Achievements are routinely recognized and celebrated. The training plan has been successfully deployed. Employee feedback is gathered through surveys, focus groups etc. Performance objectives are built into performance evaluation programs or compensation systems to support accountability.	

In this example, one issue could be that employees and management have minimal understanding of supply chain planning best practices. Therefore, the team agrees that the following actions could solve this problem:

1. Sponsor high potential employees and management to obtain supply chain management certification.

2. Hire employees with experience in organizations with highly capable supply chains.

These improvements become the start of the roadmap required to build capability. Once this assessment has been repeated for all domains, your organization will have a robust list of initiatives required to get to the next level. Then, project prioritization techniques (described in a later chapter) can be leveraged to prioritize these projects in a consistent and standardized manner.

Below is my model with characteristics for each remaining domain, and at each capability level. With your current organization in mind, review the characteristics at each level and circle the level that best describes your organization currently. You have now taken the first few steps towards building a strategic roadmap!

One important note is to understand the difference between **Capability** and **Performance**. It is quite possible that your supply chain is *performing* very well, but that does not mean that it is *capable*. Is it performing well because of constant heroics from your team? Although it's performing now, is it sustainable? What if demand were to double—could your supply chain withstand this extra test? In fact, the best time to assess your supply chain and improve its capability is when it is performing. When results are not so good, your team will be in constant "firefighting" mode and likely will not have time for a comprehensive assessment program. Take the opportunity to assess your capability when things are going well; that is fantastic. However, it is more likely that there are risks within your supply chain that you want to discover sooner rather than later.

Supply Chain Planning Capability Model

Domain	Demand Planning
Level	**Description**
1	Minimal or inconsistent use of demand planning practices. No formal policies. Significant forecast bias exists. Forecasting purely based upon shipment history. Ship dates, not customer-requested delivery date, used. Sales team has not taken ownership for the forecasting process. Demand variation is not understood. No formal process for developing the forecast. No forecast accuracy metrics. On time delivery versus original promise date is less than 80%.
2	Forecasts are developed monthly considering multiple external and internal factors, not just historical demand. Trends, seasonality, promotions are built into forecasts as needed. Quantitative and qualitative methods used as appropriate. Root cause of forecast bias is under investigation and progress is being made to reduce it. Forecasts stay at aggregate level for as long as possible. Forecasts are unconstrained by supply limitations. Demand variation has been quantified to improve safety stocks optimization.
3	Sales team has taken ownership of forecasting at the required level of detail, frequency, interval and horizon. Structured steps are utilized to develop forecasts. One consensus forecast is used by the whole organization. Effective forecast consumption techniques routinely used. Effective demand control processes including ATP/CTP, and managing abnormal demand, are prioritized. Forecasts available in units and $. Major events are documented so history is filtered. Statistical forecasts are an input not an output. Multiple sources for demand plans. Items stratified using ABC analysis to guide which items to focus on.
4	Written policies and processes covering process, roles, and responsibilities exist, are authorized by top management, and used to manage the business. Initial attempts to obtain key customer demand data. Monthly demand consensus review meetings conducted by sales and marketing management. Assumptions, risks, and opportunities are clearly communicated and used to create demand range. Gaps between demand plan and business plan are proactively managed.
5	Variation reduction techniques are utilized for understanding the root cause of forecast errors, and minimizing their impact. Assembly to order reduces needs for mix forecasts. Proration and aggregation techniques utilized to simplify mix/volume reconciliation. Demand variation is routinely measured to determine safety stock levels. The cause of difference between statistical and actual forecast is clearly understood as a sanity check. Forecast assumptions are routinely reviewed and validated.
6	Customers routinely communicate their order schedules and future demand plans. Processes and rules of operation have been agreed on and documented and are used to drive the relationship. Information is shared and leveraged with key customers. Demand influencing activities take place to help organizations meet their objectives.

Domain	Supply Planning
Level	**Description**
1	Minimal or inconsistent use of supply planning practices such as planning time fences and capacity constraints. No formal policies. Informal priority lists such as hot lists are widely used. Inventory value metrics only; inventory turns not calculated. Inventory reduction firefighting at the end of each quarter. Generic safety stock levels not adjusted for demand or lead time variation. Minimal or in-effective capacity planning. Inventory carrying costs not defined. Past due master schedule, work orders, purchase orders, planned orders.
2	The plan considers all sources of demand. Planning time fences have been established based upon cumulative lead times. Item level: firm plans exist within the PTF, volume level after PTF. Plan is constrained by capacity using RCCP/CRP, if applicable. Past due orders are under control. Distribution Requirements Planning is utilized where applicable to plan the supply chain network. Safety stocks updated to account for demand and lead time variation. SKU-level design inventory levels defined. Gaps between actual and design inventory analyzed, root cause identified, and mitigation plans developed.
3	System generates accurate exception messages that are reviewed and resolved quickly. Past due schedules routinely rescheduled. Minimal overdue messages. Effective component availability checking mechanism before order release. Operations and suppliers are accountable to meet scheduled due dates, daily run rates, Kanban requirements. Regular meetings held between production and planning to maintain valid schedules. Mitigation plans to address actual versus design inventory levels have been deployed. Blanket purchase orders are utilized where possible.
4	Written policies and processes covering purpose, process, roles and responsibilities for supply planning processes exist, are authorized by top management, and are used to manage the business. Postponement/assemble to order is utilized where practical, or routinely evaluated. Planning Bills of Materials are utilized where appropriate. VMI utilized where possible. SKU-level ideal inventory levels developed. Inventory carrying costs are defined and utilized for order size engineering. The number of exception messages for each planner is monitored for activity, trends and volumes.
5	Gaps between design and ideal inventory levels understood and actions taken to resolve including supplier negotiations for raw materials and manufacturing process constraints for finished goods. Supplier schedules are utilized and commitment zones are established representing firm material and capacity commitments. Regular meetings with key suppliers to maintain valid schedule.
6	Supply planning is fully integrated with key supply chain partners, who are committed to short lead times and quick response. Supplier base consolidation is mostly complete. Key manufacturing process constraints largely removed. CPFR, QRP, or CR programs utilized where appropriate to expedite customer response. Long-term supplier agreements for all key suppliers have eliminated the need for traditional purchase orders. Ideal inventory levels reached for more than 90% of items.

Domain	Sale & Operations Planning
Level	Description
1	S&OP is not practiced. Top management is generally unaware of S&OP benefits. Demand and Supply Planning is a non-integrated process, resulting in missed customer deliveries, expediting, higher supply chain costs, low flexibility and responsiveness, high inventory levels, financial surprises and focus on blame, not collaboration. Business planning is a time-consuming process, and plans are often missed. Few aligned objectives and measures.
2	Initial attempts to launch S&OP. Focus is on short term issues, tactical decisions and balancing supply/demand. Led by middle management. Participants are compliant, but skeptical; still not working as a team. Minimal finance involvement. Integrated KPI's have been initiated. RCCP is utilized to assess if sufficient capacity to meet demand. Demand and supply teams have collaborated to develop inventory and delivery lead time targets.
3	S&OP has become established and is led by executive management. Sales and operations teams work collaboratively. Product, Demand and Supply Management are much more integrated. A calendar of activities is mostly followed, and are scheduled 12 months out. Meeting participation is at least 90%, and only people participating in decisions attend the meeting. Reviews are focused on exceptions and making key decisions, not report outs. Focus is 80% outside and 20% inside. Bottom-up challenging top down.
4	Written policies and processes covering process, roles and responsibilities exist, are authorized by top management, and are used to manage the business. Consensus is routinely achieved on a single operating pan. Standard forms are used for communicating all issues, decisions and recommendations. Approved supply plan is truly the driver of manufacturing plan. NPI projects are reviewed to determine if they are on track.
5	S&OP is used to create the annual planning process, which has become much less time consuming. Gaps between business plan and current plan are routinely identified and addressed. Performance to date and projected performance are reviewed and robust action plans address gaps.
6	Demand, supply and financial plans are synchronized and executed as planned for 18+ months, and decisions yield the best financial performance for the company. S&OP integrated with scenario planning. Scenario Planning and modeling helps to optimize plans. Strategic customer alliances focused on long term objectives and plans. Product portfolio is compared to strategic goals, actions identified to address gaps.

Domain	Technology
Level	**Description**
1	Minimal usage of ERP systems to develop demand, supply and inventory plans. Minimal integration with external supply partners. Difficulty in obtaining data from the system. Disparate systems of record (SOR). Manual data entry predominates. Minimal efforts to improve data accuracy.
2	ERP system has been evaluated and meets 80% of needs "out of the box". Twenty percent of needs met via customization. ERP system is utilized inconsistently for demand, supply and inventory planning. Data can be easily exported from ERP system to perform analysis for decision making and KPI's.
3	ERP system is widely used for planning all products and BOM levels. Supply chain data is internally shared seamlessly and in a timely manner. Data communication methods such as EDI are utilized for high volume transactions with supply chain partners. Data accuracy is improved using data cleansing, normalization, role-based access. Initial usage of business intelligence tools to analyze and communicate key planning data and KPI's.
4	Advanced Planning and Scheduling systems (APS) used to perform optimization or simulation on finite capacity scheduling, resource planning, forecasting, network planning, etc. Automated identification systems (AIS) e.g., barcodes, RFID used to automate tracking of goods across the supply chain. Point of Sales (POS) systems share sales data immediately throughout the supply chain.
5	Advanced graphical and analytical tools are used. Dashboards become customizable and mobile. Supply Chain Execution Management (SCEM) monitors, measures, notifies, simulates and controls real time events to enable faster response times. Data shared externally in real time using straight-through processing for tracking materials, products and providing exception alerts.
6	User-friendly, fully functional ERP system that integrates the entire network of trading partners. Electronic integration with supply chain partners. WMS, TMS CRM, SRM utilized where appropriate. Big data utilized where appropriate such as demand sensing and demand shaping. B2B commerce creates faster communication.

| Domain | Metrics |
Level	Description
1	Ill-defined metrics, ownership or accountability. Metrics data used for reporting and compliance purposes only. Management expects metric data to be "green," so there is defensiveness and gaming of the metrics. Targets set low enough to ensure they are "green." Meetings where performance is discussed are "report outs" rather than decision-making forums.
2	Purpose of metrics is clarified to drive better business decisions and take action. Focused efforts on improving critical data accuracy such as forecasts, inventory record, BOM, routings, manufacturing schedule adherence and supplier on time delivery. Organizational alignment on key inventory performance metrics, typically inventory turns and on-time delivery, versus original promise or requested date.
3	Metric definitions become consistent across the organization. When targets are not met, the organization embraces the results and engages in a healthy debate to decide what action is needed to improve performance. Measure on-time order customer delivery, manufacturing adhere to plan, on-time supplier delivery and inventory turns.
4	Written policies and processes covering process, roles and responsibilities exist, are authorized by top management, and are used to manage the business. Metrics are aligned with corporate and supply chain goals. Detailed specs exist for all metrics. Performance versus targets is consistently assessed at operational review meetings. These meetings are decision-making meetings and focused on process improvement, not finger-pointing.
5	Targets are set based upon multiple sources: historical trend, benchmark, business goals. Targets are segmented by supply chain. Individual and group incentives are aligned toward supply chain performance. Measure on-time delivery and inventory turns by supply chain segment.
6	Metrics and targets now span the entire network of trading partners. Perfect order metric is now the focus (complete, on-time, accurate, in perfect condition). Inventory turns have improved 4-10X, 30-60% reduction in manufacturing space, 50-90% reduction in throughput times. Compliance audits are conducted as needed.

Domain Level	Lean Description
1	Long lead times, low inventory turns, large batches, long setups, poor quality, many inspections. Lots of firefighting; problems frequently occur, and root cause is rarely identified. Push inventory replenishment, not pull. Minimal visual management. People's ideas are generally not solicited. Transactional supplier relationships where focus is on price, not total cost. Large supply base.
2	Top management actively supports a lean transformation and understands the required commitment. Value stream mapping activities have identified opportunities to increase velocity. Initial steps taken to reduce waste, lead times, variability, inventory, set ups via Kaizen events. Daily inventory management has been established.
3	Visual management has made problems more visible. A continuous improvement mindset has become more prevalent. Cell manufacturing and Kanban pilot has been successfully completed. People's ideas are encouraged and put into practice. Accomplishments are recognized. Root cause analysis techniques employed to effectively solve problems.
4	Cellular manufacturing, Kanban, Hejunka/mixed model scheduling have been implemented where applicable. Standard work established. Work orders and purchase orders have been eliminated or minimized. Firm schedule days are being reduced. Supplier base consolidation and single sourcing has been initiated. Frequent Kaizen events. Warehouse storage density has been evaluated and improved.
5	Long term supplier relationships are established. Efficiencies such as removing incoming inspection, no PO's, returnable containers, and frequent POU deliveries are being realized. Level loaded releases. Focus is on lowest cost, not price. Cross-docking opportunities exploited to increase velocity and reduce handling.
6	Product design includes early supplier involvement, standardization, component commonality, modularization, universality, simplification, concurrent engineering, design for quality. Buyers now focused on developing supplier relationships. Decisions are shared, not handed down.

Chapter 6

Phase 3:
Bridge the Gaps,
Steps 1 and 2

"If everything seems under control, you're not going fast enough."

–Mario Andretti

I n the earlier chapters, the focus was on mining the gaps. As these gaps are identified we must develop solutions to bridge the gaps. We can start to bridge the gaps as we continue to mine them—the two phases can be worked on in parallel. This is critical since it could take several years to complete all the steps of the *Mine the Gaps* phase. Obviously, no organization has the patience to wait that long to start seeing results.

Since there will likely be no shortages of gaps, it can be overwhelming to know where to start. Which solutions should we prioritize, and which ones should we discard? In many companies with immature project prioritization practices, each department makes its own decisions with minimal input at the organizational level. While local decision-making may be valid, having different processes and criteria for making decisions is not. Maybe there are a handful of key projects that have organization-level visibility, but most projects are selected and managed in silos. If this is the case at your company, not to worry—you are not alone.

Step 1: Escalate Transformation

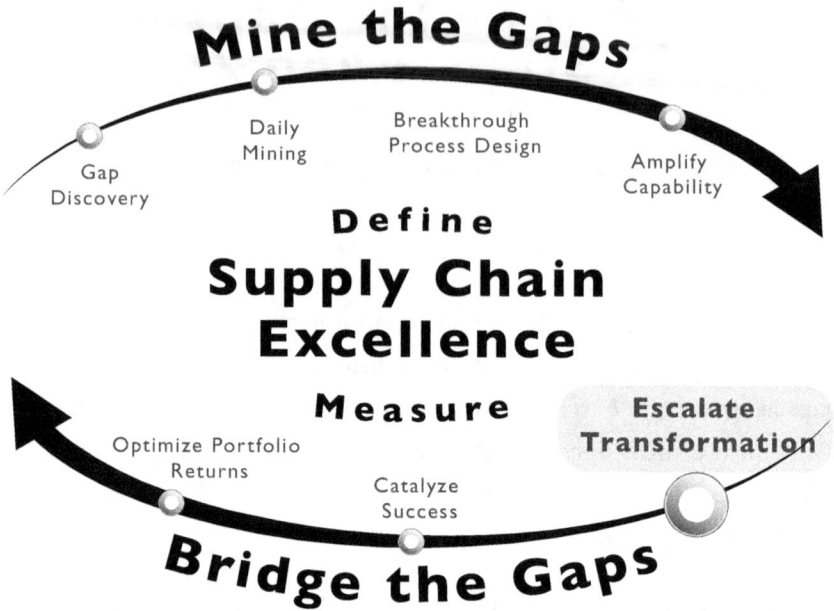

To Escalate Transformation, we will use a simple matrix to rank possible solutions to bridge the gaps based on their impact and effort on your selected metric(s).

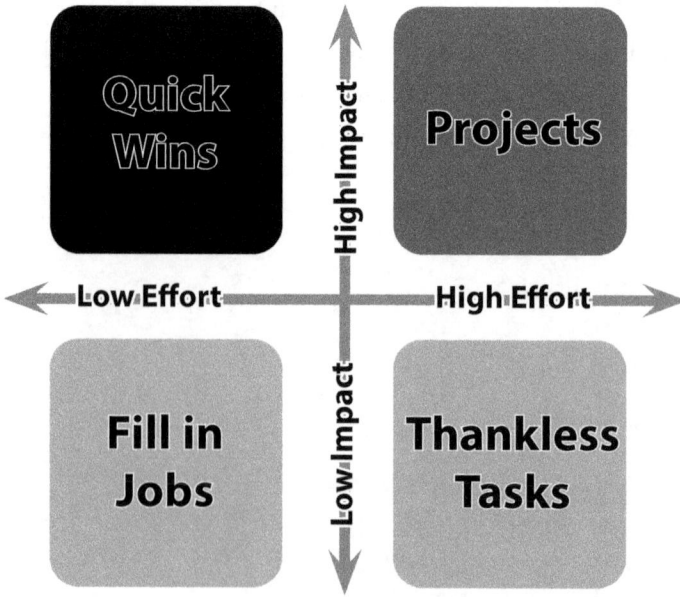

Each possible solution is scored on a scale of 1-5 based on the expected impact of the solution and the level of effort required to implement it. Here, "impact" is measured by how much the solution will move the needle on your selected metric. (Ideally, from the previous root cause analysis you can quantify the impact.) "Effort" should be estimated in terms of labor hours, project duration, technology required, cost and cross-functional alignment required. A word of caution here: Don't spend too much time developing these criteria; you can refine them later. The important thing is to start using a well-defined structure.

Those solutions deemed to be above the horizontal line, i.e., *High Impact*, will have the highest priority. However, to make quick progress, identify those that are *Low Effort* and implement them first. These *Quick Wins* (aka low-hanging fruit) should be completed without delay. Since they do not require much effort, resource planning is unnecessary. On the other hand, *Projects* should be analyzed for resource requirements and availability. We will look at how to manage project portfolios in the next chapter.

These *Quick Wins* will immediately build your credibility. This will be very helpful in the long term as you tackle some of the more challenging gaps.

Step 2: Catalyze Success

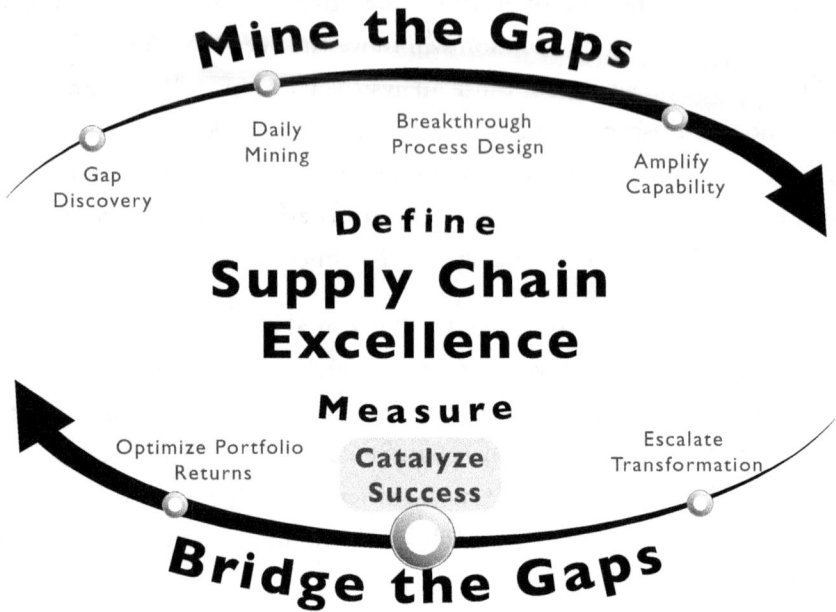

One approach to *Catalyze Success* is to hold **Kaizen events**. During these events, a team dedicates a few days to addressing a specific and important business challenge by applying operational excellence tools.

Kaizen events are like projects on steroids. I'm sure that we have all suffered through never-ending projects that seem to last forever. The initiative often runs out of steam before benefits are realized. Although team members may have good ideas on how to address an issue, it often never happens. Generally, it is difficult to get all the necessary players to align on improvements. It requires a concerted effort to translate the idea into a solution that everyone is aligned with, and most solutions take effort to implement. Kaizen events, however, are condensed projects so you can achieve your objectives much more effectively and quickly with this approach. The Kaizen event creates the opportunity for team members to work together to operationalize the improvement.

Kaizen events should be driven by a specific business need linked to a strategic objective. Kaizen events take significant resources, so they should be carefully selected. Kaizen objectives should also be aggressive, which will encourage creative thinking. By thinking more boldly, the team is more likely to achieve transformational results, such as:

- ➤ Reduce lead time by 50%
- ➤ Reduce WIP by 70%
- ➤ Improve productivity by 25%
- ➤ Reduce setup time by 50%

While capital-intensive solutions are sometimes the best ones, this is not always the case, so they should not be the first resort. In many cases, simple common sense tools can make all the difference without the need to open your wallet. Be sure to favor action over analysis. Whenever possible, the changes should be implemented during the Kaizen event itself. If doing so is not possible, rigorous follow up is required to ensure that the remaining actions are completed.

There are a few things to keep in mind when implementing a Kaizen culture within your organization. To minimize resistance from your team, it is very important to have employee involvement in the development of the future state from the outset, not after the design has been developed. Instead of feeling like something is being done to them, employees will have energy and enthusiasm for the changes. This is what makes Kaizen events so powerful. Employees at different levels and in different departments participate in the redesign efforts.

In a Kaizen culture, the organization is striving for perfection. Obviously, this will never be achieved, but it doesn't mean that you will not continuously strive for it. Eventually this mindset will be ingrained within the fabric of the company and will become second nature to everyone. That is the goal.

KAIZEN CHARTER

The starting point of any Kaizen event is a charter. It should include the following key elements:

➤ *Strategic Objective*: Which strategic objective will be impacted?

➤ *Problem Statement*: A quantified definition of why the Kaizen is necessary. This should show the business impact and scope (e.g., which sites, products, etc.)

➤ *Targets*: What is the current performance level and what level of improvement is expected, and by when?

➤ *Deliverables*: What will be the tangible outputs such as documents, layout redesign, etc.?

➤ *Executive Sponsor*: Which member of the senior management team is responsible for the strategic objective and is the internal advocate for the Kaizen event?

➤ *Pre-work*: Before all Kaizen events, some work will be required. This is typically the collection of data that will help us better understand the problem in question.

There are three stages to keep in mind for all Kaizen events:

1. Assess (current state)

2. Architect (plan the improvement)

3. Achieve (make the change)

Before the project starts, it is a good practice to set ground rules. Here are some examples:

- ➤ Treat others as you'd like to be treated
- ➤ Keep an open mind
- ➤ Maintain a positive attitude
- ➤ Never leave in silent disagreement
- ➤ Create a safe environment
- ➤ Practice mutual respect
- ➤ One person, one voice—no position or rank
- ➤ There is no such thing as a dumb question
- ➤ Understand the process
- ➤ Just do it!

If the Kaizen event will require new, specific skills or tools, there is no better time to train the team than at the beginning of the Kaizen event. The training should be focused upon the specific tools that will likely be required for that event so the relevance is obvious. By providing training so close to when the skill or tool is required, the team gets to apply their knowledge very soon after learning it.

Finally, it is important that the executive sponsor be available for the kick-off to encourage the team. In addition, there should be daily report outs so that the sponsor can ask questions and remove obstacles, if necessary. One of the worst things that could possibly happen is that the team does not receive any feedback until the end of the Kaizen. Then, the sponsor sees the results, and tells the team that they are way off the mark. Nothing will kill enthusiasm quicker than this situation. It is better to find out immediately if you are off-track, while there is still time to course correct.

Now that we have covered the quicker bridge-building practices, the next chapter will focus on projects that require more time and resources.

Mine the Gaps

Chapter 7

Phase 3:
Bridge the Gaps,
Step 3

"We cannot solve our problems with the same level of thinking that created them."

–Albert Einstein

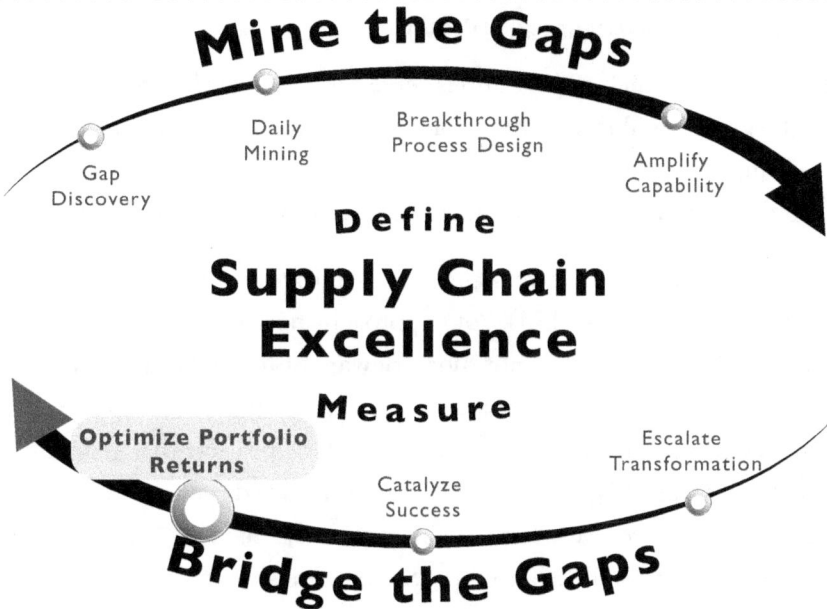

A large global corporation conducted a study that showed that 45% of their projects contributed only 2% of the value of their overall project portfolio[1] (Menard, 2012). They are not alone. Imagine the time and effort wasted on these projects that added little value. How does this happen? Simply put, project prioritization is not a process for many companies. Projects are often selected in a haphazard manner, so it is not entirely surprising that the results are not acceptable. In addition, even when the right projects are selected, they are frequently not executed effectively, so the intended benefits are not realized.

---

1   Menard, M. (2012). A fish in your ear: The new discipline of project portfolio management. CreateSpace.

Where to Start?

"In the earlier chapters the focus was on mining the gaps." As these gaps were identified, we developed solutions to bridge them. We started by differentiating the *Quick Wins* from the *Projects*, which take more time and resources. With this done, how do we now decide which projects to tackle first, and which ones not to bother with? In this chapter, we will focus on how to effectively manage the project portfolio to optimize returns.

PROJECT PORTFOLIO MANAGEMENT (PPM)

PPM is choosing which opportunities serve the needs of the organization and deliver the greatest value. It is the deployment of finite resources to maximize return on investment (ROI) in the long term. Project portfolio management will help you decide what to do and, equally as important, what *not* to do.

The first step is to categorize your projects as ones that deliver growth and others that keep the lights on (KTLO). Your approach should be to work on all the necessary KTLO projects, but not more. Beware of those department heads that want to consider all their projects as "KTLO"—use the definition sparingly and intelligently. Next, ensure that you also include projects that generate growth. Analysis of a Fortune 500 corporation revealed that only 13% of the organization's resources were focused on growth (Menard, 2012). This is not unusual. As with any well-balanced portfolio, there should be a good mix of high risk, high return and low risk, low return projects. In other words, the portfolio should be balanced between growth and maintenance.

To assess the value of your current project portfolio, establish a standardized process, which will keep you from reinventing the wheel. Unless project selection is seen as a process rather than an event, we are likely to jump to the conclusion that any action is right. Without a process to guide us we can be swayed by many factors, some seen and some unseen. Process keeps us on track by reminding us of what is relevant. As stated by author and management consultant W. Edwards Deming, "If you can't describe what you are doing as a process, you don't know what you're doing." Project valuation, prioritization, and selection need to take place in a holistic environment where the likely impact and interdependencies of these processes can be understood, and then evaluated in the context of the whole. Otherwise, you are left with an ad hoc decision-making process, which cannot consider the ripple effect of its actions on other business units or the organization. In such a fragmented decision-making environment, not only will the processes vary, but decisions will rest on diverse criteria. This is the exact opposite of the holistic PPM approach.

Instead, I suggest developing a scoring model to prioritize projects, but I want you to keep it simple. Do not overthink the model. I once served a life science company that took over six months to define criteria to score the importance of their projects. Please do not overcomplicate this step! After you have judiciously segregated the KTLO projects, select a few drivers that are meaningful to the organization and weigh them accordingly. Here are a few sample drivers you could use:

➤ Alignment to strategy

➤ ROI

➤ Compliance

➤ Growth

Next, rate the impact of each project against these drivers (High, Medium, Low) so each project now has a score. Take the model for a test drive by scoring a handful of projects to see if it generates credible prioritization and modify as necessary. A word of caution is called for here. Our goal is to get an unbiased assessment from information providers. If we make public the relative importance of each driver, then projects will not be scored honestly. It is better to keep knowledge of the weighting to a "need to know basis."

Note that when assessing your current portfolio, you will generally find that 20% of projects will receive about 80% of the total score (A projects). Does this sound familiar? You will also likely find that 50% of projects will only receive 5% of the total score (C projects).

A PROJECTS

These projects should be prioritized to ensure that they have sufficient resources. The first step then is to estimate the resource requirements per month for each of these projects to see if any potential constraints exist. If so, get them resolved immediately. There should be a regular review of these projects, governance should be enforced, etc.

B PROJECTS

These projects will comprise 30% of projects and receive about 15% of the total score. Once resources have been allocated to the A projects, then resources can be allocated to B projects starting with the ones with the highest score. Once you start to hit against resource constraints, seriously consider stopping those projects. Otherwise, you will be pulling resources from higher priority projects.

C PROJECTS

Your organization should seriously consider halting these projects unless there is a compelling reason not to do so. This presents an enormous opportunity for most life science organizations. Why? Because except for money spent on making and selling products, almost all of a company's resources are spent on projects. In a life science organization, I estimate that at least 50% of your employees' time is spent working on projects of some sort. Therefore, even by canceling just the 50% of projects that yield only 5% of your portfolio's total value, you will increase your project ROI by 2X. Once the other benefits of project portfolio management described earlier are added, the ROI improvement should be even greater. So, what are you waiting for?

PROJECT MANAGEMENT

Once you know that you are working on the *right things*, it is time to *do these right things right* by effectively managing your projects. There are many books out there on project management practices, so I will not spend too much time on them here. However, I would like to spend some time emphasizing the importance of well-defined deliverables.

A well-defined set of project deliverables is one of the keys to success on any project. They convert the project objectives into something tangible. Without these deliverables, the project outputs are unclear. To ascertain whether a deliverable is a good one, use the Done/Not Done test. You should be able to ask whether a deliverable is done or not and get a clear "yes" or "no." The answer should not be "almost," "mostly," or "it's 64.67% done." In this case, it will be much easier to claim that the deliverables have been completed when they really have not been. This can happen frequently on life science supply chain projects, where there is often some Quality Assurance (QA) validation or release process that is required before an action can be considered complete. On many occasions, I have seen a deliverable be described prematurely as "100% complete" when it still has not been QA evaluated. Here are key questions about the deliverables to ask yourself before you start your next project:

Is it clear what "done" looks like?

To avoid lots of rework and frustration, create clarity in this area. If "done" is not clearly defined, then it is easy to fool yourself and others that a deliverable is complete when it really is not.

Do you know the phase in which the deliverable must be completed?

Unless it is clearly understood what should be completed, and in which phase, it is quite easy to mistakenly allow the project to pass through the phase-gate.

Are deliverables aligned with project objectives?

If you waved a magic wand and all the deliverables were suddenly available, would the project realize its intended benefits, or would something else still be missing? Conversely, are there deliverables not contributing to the project objectives? If so, remove them from the project scope.

Deliverables also facilitate the development of a project plan. They can be utilized as the basis for identification of the tasks required. In addition, they can be used to structure the project plan, with each task stemming from each deliverable. This is called a work breakdown structure (WBS). For example, when building a house the deliverables could be defined by function: plumbing, electric power, etc. or by room: kitchen, main bedroom, bathroom, etc... There is no right answer to how you structure the project if the sum of the deliverables meets the objectives. For example, you don't want to omit a room or function in the project plan, nor do you want to include a deliverable for three bathrooms when the scope was for only two.

ERP Implementation Project Turnaround

Here is an example of how we leveraged deliverables to turnaround a large, failing ERP project. Many of you have probably been through an ERP implementation. Do you still wake up in a cold sweat thinking about it? I have heard it likened to a "corporate root canal"—something that nobody enjoys at the time, but which should make life less painful eventually.

This ERP project was for a biotech company transitioning from clinical to commercial stage. We were contacted halfway through the project because the steering committee had serious concerns about how it was being managed. We were able to get the project back on track. At the end of the project, we were asked to perform a "lessons learned" exercise to identify reasons that it had been continuously delayed versus meeting the original baseline dates (see table below):

Phase	Weeks Delayed
Discovery	0
Design	2
Build	23
Validation	21
Deploy	26

As you can see from the table, the significant delays to the project did not occur until the "build" phase. The reason for this is that deliverables that were supposed to be completed in the discovery and design phases were not truly completed. You can hide the impact of the incomplete deliverables in the earlier phases of the project. However, if a solid foundation has not been designed, the delays will become visible in the build phase.

To avoid this issue, business processes must be defined and have cross-functional alignment early in the design phase. In addition, the functional subject matter experts (SMEs) should all be proficient with their transactions. They must be capable enough to pass a hands-on test before the build phase begins.

For this project, that was not the case at all. In fact, even at the end of the design phase, business processes had not yet been defined. In addition, SMEs were still lacking a basic understanding of their transactions. In other words, the build phase began with a very weak foundation, including ill-defined business processes and untrained SMEs.

The way we turned this project around was by increasing the focus on the deliverables. Immediately after taking charge of the project, we made several changes:

➤ For each deliverable, we clarified "what done looks like" to reduce the frustration caused by rework and delays. In life science organizations, it is often the Quality Assurance group that decides the documentation requirements for deliverables in a Good Manufacturing Practice (GMP) environment. In this case, QA had extremely specific and rigorous requirements, which were often not understood. It was not until the deliverable got close to the due date that it became clear there was misalignment. We changed this process so that the team had these conversations before work started on each deliverable.

➤ We held a series of cross-functional workshops for each business process such as Receive to QA Release, Internal Production Control, Item and BOM management, etc. The purpose of these workshops was to obtain alignment on the business process design. In addition, they increased accountability and visibility for SMEs since we frequently performed informal Conference Room Pilots. During these sessions, the team was responsible for performing their transactions in sequence.

➤ We assessed the scope versus project benefits to determine if there was an opportunity to reduce scope. As a result, we removed finished goods supply chain planning from the project scope since the company only had two active finished goods. The complexity and training required to create a robust supply chain plan in the ERP system was not worth it. The plan could easily continue to be generated in Excel and transitioned to ERP in the future. This scope reduction increased the likelihood that the team would be ready on time.

These changes had an immediate positive impact. Even though accountability was now much higher, team morale improved significantly. This was because progress was finally being made and they weren't wasting their time in endless meetings. These were simple changes that resulted in big wins for the company. And although it was late, when the ERP system was eventually implemented, it was launched with very few hitches. The project was highly acclaimed by senior executives, especially the CFO who was the project sponsor.

Chapter 8

Case Study
Part 1: Mine the Gaps

"We cannot become what we want by remaining what we are."

–Max Depree

Hopefully, you now know how to mine the gaps and then how to bridge them. In this chapter, I will show how the concepts and practices shared in this book can be operationalized in the real world. In fact, I have leveraged this approach many times throughout my career to achieve strategic goals (see examples on the next page).

We will take a deep dive into specific case studies from two previous clients to provide comprehensive examples of each step within the framework. To keep things simple, I have presented both examples as if they were one company and one case study.

Situation

This life science company had grown very quickly over the past few years and had unfortunately outgrown their supply chain systems. They manufactured bioanalytical instruments and the consumables required to operate them, such as reagents and cartridges. In addition, they supplied spare parts to the field service team to maintain and replace failed instrument parts.

Each of their key product categories—instruments, spare parts and consumables—had poor on-time delivery performance. Each quarter, it was a dash to the finish line to meet revenue targets. Customers were far from happy about all the delays, and the sales team was losing faith. It was under these circumstances that the management team asked me to intervene. The situation was perfectly set up to follow the *Mind the Gaps* methodology.

Mine the Gaps Use Cases

Strategic Objective	Key gaps	Solutions	Results
Reduce product recalls due to assembly errors	Material handling errors Assemblers distracted by multiple tasks	Reduced material touches by 80% Assemblers dedicated to one task—Assembly	50% assembly error reduction
Reduce warehouse labor costs	Random stocking locations for kit components	Create "supermarket" for high volume kits so all components stored together	28% reduction in minutes per pick
Warehouse cost avoidance	Excess packaging inventory Insufficient rack space utilization	Packaging supplier kanban Add smaller storage space options	100% reduction in overflow pallets 30% improved space utilization
Reduce logistics costs	Modal suboptimization, load techniques, LTL carrier selection	Intermodal verses over the road, regional pool verses LTL, Truckloading software	$4.4M logistics costs savings per year
Reduce excess and obsolete inventory	Sales team request speculative purchases	Formal executive management approval process	Reduced E&O inventory by 84%
Improve material management compliance	Excess, obsolete procedures used for training material handlers	Consolidate and maintain procedures to use as training tools	Reduced procedure documents from 100+ to six
Improved Revenue Attainment	Component shortages preventing production of instruments	Rigorous kanban system, supply agreements, level loaded production	Reduced shippable backlog value by 62%
Improved customer service	Miscommunication of product launch dates Inaccurate transit times	Launch date maintenance, consolidate carriers, formal transit times	Improve OTD from 80% to 99% in four months
ERP based supply chain planning	Software functionality gaps, transaction delays, bill of material inaccuracies	Reconfigured software, transactional training, develop BOM accuracy report	% items planning in ERP increased from 0% to 95%
Improved forecast accuracy	Items with high demand and variance, inconsistent forecast communication	Collaboration with key customers, develop monthly demand review	15% forecast accuracy improvement

Phase 1: Step 1– Strategic Objective

It was clear that the key strategic objective was **to better serve their customers with higher on-time delivery performance**. Further discussions with the commercial team made it clear that it was the *consumable items* that were the highest priority—even above the *instruments* which provided the bulk of the revenue. Once a lab had switched to the client's instrument, it was committed and, therefore, required their consumables to run the instrument. If the consumables were not available, this could delay an experiment, which would really frustrate the customer. Similarly, spare parts were generally ordered to correct an instrument failure, so again, this product category impacted a customer's ability to do their work. On the other hand, before the customer received the instruments, they were still using the previous method so their work would not be delayed. Due to their revenue impact, instrument backorders were more likely to upset the salesperson and senior management.

Phase 1: Step 2 – Level 2 Metric

Following my framework, the next step was to select the key metric. In this case, it was on-time delivery (OTD). Since this was a current, active metric, we decided to keep the same calculation. In this way, we could easily measure progress relative to historical performance. Some argued about the technicalities of how the metric was calculated. While their arguments had some merit, I did not want to waste time defining a new metric. The focus should be on making improvements because changing the way that performance is measured would not move the needle.

It is always a good practice to clearly define key elements of the metric, otherwise it will be measured and interpreted differently throughout the organization. In this case, we developed the following metric specification.

Metric	Customer On Time Delivery
Description	Measure of how consistently we meet our delivery commitments to our customers
Calculation	% Order line items delivered by the commit date
In Scope	Order type: Instruments, consumables, internal, and repairs. Site: San Francisco, CA
Out of Scope	Order type: Service orders
Responsible	Senior Supply Chain Manager
Metric Owner	Senior Director, Operations
Publish Frequency	Weekly
Target	98%
Data Source	Accounts Receivable Detail Report

A senior member of the commercial team approved all these details, to ensure that our specifications met customer expectations.

PHASE 2: STEP 1 – GAP DISCOVERY

Once management settled on the metric, the next step was to use defect data to find the gaps preventing us from achieving the 98% target. To perform this analysis, we formed a cross-functional team including planning, purchasing, shipping, manufacturing, order management, quality, and the commercial team. These were all groups that could impact the selected metric. The team agreed that the defect data in this case would be late customer orders. Fortunately (or unfortunately) over 300 customer order lines were backordered so there was no shortage of data to sample. Next, we held a workshop to review these backorders and to define the reason for the delays.

Within 90 minutes, we had found chronic issues that had been around for years. The workshop was a little painful because we carefully reviewed each order. However, since we had all the right people in the room, we agreed upon the reason for 82% of the line items by the end of the workshop. The key gaps found by the team could be grouped into two categories: order management (OM) and stock-outs.

Order Management

Order management-related issues referred to errors in the sales order data, not inventory availability issues. Interestingly, about two-thirds of the late lines were in this category. The team suspected it was high, but did not think it was close to this number. The specific errors included:

Commit Dates

Even though every product had a standard lead time, the OM team often did not consider it when they entered the order. Since it was all a manual process, it was not surprising there were so many errors. The Planners also maintained a list of items that had longer lead times than the standard, but OM often missed these exceptions. The result was that OM gave the customer an inaccurate commit date and OTD performance was severely impacted.

Internal Orders

These were orders placed by internal employees, such as R&D and engineers, some of which had been placed over six months prior. For these orders, the product was typically available on time but whoever had placed the order had not picked it up. The team agreed that these orders were "noise" and should not impact the on-time shipment metric.

Customer Carrier

In these cases, the product was available, but the customer's carrier was delayed in picking up the order. For this category, it was also agreed that they should not impact the on-time shipment metric.

On Hold

These orders were on credit hold when the order was supposed to ship, so even though the product was available, they could not ship it.

Shipping Schedule

The issue here was primarily related to international orders. International customers had fixed shipping days each week. Since the transportation costs were high to reach these destinations, it made economic sense to consolidate shipments. However, order management often did not consider the ship day when establishing the commit date. For example, maybe they only shipped to Germany on Thursdays. If one of the orders was placed on a Friday and given a commit date of the following Monday, they could not ship on time regardless of whether the inventory was available.

Stock-outs

Once we filtered out the order management issues, we were left with one-third of the late orders. For these items, the high-level reason the orders were late was that the product was not available when the order was due to ship. Obviously, we needed to know why the order was not on the shelf. We found several gaps:

Product quality

First, we found that many orders were late due to a bulk batch for which there were quality concerns. Even though the batch had been completed several weeks earlier, it still had not been resolved. Interestingly, the reason given was that the scientist most familiar with this product was on vacation. By asking more questions, however, we discovered that several other people had the knowledge but had not been contacted.

Next, we discovered that one of the frozen raw materials used to manufacture the bulk item had been stored in a damaged container. This was identified as the cause of the quality issue. We were then told by the scientists that it was better to discard unused quantities of raw material than to store it.

Capacity

The next cause of stock-outs was labor shortages caused by the tremendous growth the client had experienced over the past few years. We found that the "compounding" operation was experiencing a significant labor shortage, which accounted for about 60% of the capacity issues.

New products

We discovered several issues related to new products. Since there was no historical shipping data to help forecast demand, the supply chain group depended on the sales team to provide a good and timely forecast at least six months before launch. This was necessary to allow enough time to purchase long lead time raw materials that were unique to the new products. Since the demand planning process maturity was exceptionally low, these practices were absent. The forecast for the latest new product was not given to operations until two months before the planned launch date, which caused a scramble to expedite material purchases. To exacerbate the problem, the new product sold like hot cakes, so the supply chain did not catch up until several months after launch. In other words, the good news was that there was clearly demand for the new product, but the bad news was that it could not be fulfilled in a timely manner.

Expiring raw materials

Many item shortages were caused by expired raw materials, which were not tracked in the ERP system. In other words, when manufacturing picked the materials required to make a batch, they found that they had expired.

Inventory inaccuracies

The operations team found that inventory inaccuracies were a major cause of component shortages. This was a well-known problem. In fact, the buyers would frequently go into the warehouse to find an item rather than rely upon the system inventory. They would often hoard hard to find items under their desks to secure the inventory for future needs. The warehouse team performed cycle counts and a quick analysis showed that accuracy was below 70% over the past six months.

One of the client's primary issues was that there was inventory everywhere on-site, which made it difficult to find inventory when the team needed it for production. It was in the aisles of the warehouse, which caused congestion and safety hazards. They had to remove about 30 pallets of materials every day and put them outside, just to perform regular operations. Then at the end of the day, they had to be brought back in again.

Even worse, they did not track bin locations, so the ERP system just told the client that an item was somewhere in the warehouse, but not *where* in the warehouse. All these issues resulted in line down events, late customer orders, and revenue risk.

To further quantify inventory inaccuracy issues, we created a **"Control Group."** This was about 20 items that the warehouse team would count every day. The selected items were a representative sample of the total item population. Since these items were counted daily, any discrepancy would have happened in the past 24 hours, making it easy to find what caused the problem. This is different than cycle counting where even "A" items are likely to be counted no more than once per month. Since "A" items are likely to have many transactions, even the most frequently counted items will be challenging to investigate.

Once the items were selected, the team followed these steps:

1. Count all "control group" items each day;

2. Find, investigate, and fix inaccuracies;

3. Identify the root cause and note a "reason code" for each inaccuracy;

4. Identify and address the critical few root causes; and

5. Repeat the process until the client consistently achieved 95% accuracy.

After a few days, we found there were two primary issues:

1.   *Delayed system receipts*

Due to a lack of staff trained to perform inventory transactions, the transactions could be delayed for a few days, so the system inventory was misaligned with the physical inventory.

2.   *Unit of measure (UOM) discrepancies*

Before the ERP system had been implemented, the warehouse would manually track inventory in a spreadsheet. Unfortunately, in some cases, the UOM set up in the ERP system was different than the one the warehouse team had used.

Once an item had been set up in the ERP system, it was not possible to change the UOM. The warehouse team would sometimes continue to count inventory in the UOM to which they were accustomed. For example, if they had previously used liters as the UOM, but the item was set up in the ERP system with milliliters as the UOM, their count could be off by a factor of 1000.

PHASE 2: STEP 2 - DAILY MINING

Supply chains are very dynamic so, in addition to mining the data, it was necessary to keep on top of what was happening each day. Obviously the COVID-19 pandemic was a major example of this issue in action, but we all know of everyday examples, such as unforecasted customer orders or supplier delays.

The team was already meeting daily, but I was concerned about the tools and analytics that the team were using. Scheduling succeeds or fails based upon whether the team has accurate data that they interpret correctly. The data the team was initially using to schedule and prioritize was very vague and gave too much latitude for the production supervisor to build what they wanted. Indeed, when we started to measure schedule attainment, we found that it was only about 30%. Clearly, the lack of precision with the scheduling tools created a potential risk that a supply chain disruption would go unnoticed.

PHASE 2: STEP 3 – BREAKTHROUGH PROCESS DESIGN

Gap Discovery and Daily Mining has uncovered many broken business processes. For example, the introduction of new products was always a painful experience from a planning perspective. It is not unusual that an organization with a low maturity level is challenged to plan new products effectively. This makes perfect sense since existing products have some historical data to improve planning accuracy, such as sales history, production yields, bills of materials, etc... Since new products have minimal reliable planning data, they are more difficult to plan with any degree of accuracy.

My client was no different, with highly inaccurate forecasts and insufficient capacity. As with many companies, there was much pressure to launch products quickly. If that meant corners were cut to meet the launch date, so be it. There would be time post-launch to correct any problems, right? Most of you will roll your eyes at this point. Since your team is so busy putting out the fires caused by similar hurried launches, there is no time to correct the underlying issues. Instead, you repeatedly deal with the symptoms. Regardless, these premature launches continue to be pushed by senior management. Despite this, we were confident that we would find many opportunities for improvement that were within the team's control.

New Product Introduction (NPI) Process Redesign

Since NPI involves many departments, the first step was to form a cross-functional team. Given that the NPI has multiple phases and countless steps, the team's first task was to define project scope.

The client's NPI process included four phases:

Phase	Start	End
1. Feasibility	Feasibility start	Feasibility end
2. Design	Feasibility end	Design lock
3. Launch	Design lock	Launch
4. Post launch	Launch	Sustained

From a supply chain perspective, there is no real activity in Phase 1. In Phase 2, there was some supply chain related activity in selecting and approving suppliers. While the vendor selection process needed some attention, making changes to it would be a real upheaval within the organization. Supply chain planning typically starts with a demand forecast, which is generally received about the same time as design lock. Based upon this information, the team decided that the project should start with Phase 3. In addition, since supply chain plays a critical part in post-launch success, we all agreed that Phase 4 should also be in scope. In summary, the selected process was from "forecast to sustain."

The team developed the current state process map, I then asked the team to identify as many pain points as possible. These were some of the key issues they identified:

Bills of material (BOM) changes

BOMs were frequently changed after design lock, and not distributed until midway through Phase 3. This created problems for the purchasing team since they were unclear about how much to purchase for any given item.

New item/BOM creation

The complete process to add new items/formulations was very manual, causing delays and errors.

Document control system

The document control system was not well understood by the purchasing group. This was mainly because there had been high turnover in purchasing and no training program. Therefore, not only was the bill of material delivered late, but it was also possible that buyers could misinterpret the information within the document control system and send the wrong specification to a supplier.

Vendor selection

Engineering typically selected the vendors for new items and had the relationships. Since they are not purchasing professionals, they did not develop supply agreements to reduce supply risk.

Purchasing and engineering communication

Handoff from engineering to purchasing was ineffective, which led to misunderstandings between the two teams and communication errors.

Single-sourcing

The launch timeline did not allow for the qualification of two suppliers. Since there was no supply agreement with the selected supplier, there was a greater risk that parts would not be available when demand increased. That proved to be the case for their recent launch, where actual demand far exceeded the forecast, and the supplier was not able to react in time. This caused supply shortages and backorders for several months.

Demand forecast sources

Demand forecasts from the sales team excluded no charge demand for training and internal requests. At the time of launch, the no charge demand is often significant, so forecasts have an inbuilt negative bias, which can cause material shortages and delays.

Forecast timeliness

It was not unusual for the supply chain team to receive forecasts only 1-2 months before the launch date. This created lots of pressure to procure sufficient materials to avoid stock-outs at launch time.

Forecast version control

In the most recent new product introduction, the forecast was much lower than actual shipments. However, the commercial team claimed that operations were not using the latest version of the forecast. The latest version was supposed to be much higher than the original forecast that operations had been using to drive production, capacity, and material plans.

Inventory planning

Process Engineers selected reorder points and purchase order quantities, even though it was the buyers that were held accountable for part shortages. As you can imagine, this created lots of finger-pointing and made it difficult to know who was accountable for part availability.

Typically, the next step in the *Mine the Gaps* phase is "Amplify Capability." At the time of writing, this step has not been started since there are already so many opportunities in the first three steps. However, as I mentioned earlier in the book, the *Mine the Gaps* phase does not have to be completed before we bridge the gaps. Since amplifing capability is a long-term initiative, it is a good practice to start to bridge the gaps before this step.

In the next chapter, you will learn the solutions we developed to address the gaps. In addition, you will find out how we prioritized them and what the results were.

Chapter 9

Case Study
Part 2: Bridge the Gaps

"To improve is to change; to be perfect is to change often."

–Winston Churchill

PHASE 3: STEP 1 – ESCALATE TRANSFORMATION

The team set about finding the solutions that would be *highly impactful* and would require *low effort* so that they could be implemented immediately. These were known as "quick wins" or "low hanging fruit." On the other hand, if the team found solutions that would have *high impact* but required *significant effort*, these were classified as "projects." They cannot all be done at once and should be put on a road map along with other projects and prioritized.

The team brainstormed and identified many solutions. They found the following solutions to be quick wins, and set about implementing them immediately:

SOURCE: GAP DISCOVERY

Order Management issues

Gaps	Solution
Inaccurate commit dates	Automate assignment of commit dates based upon product type
Internal orders impacting OTD	Assign a dummy due date that would not impact OTD calculations
Delayed customer carrier pick up	Move out commit date by two weeks in these instances
Orders on hold cannot ship	Create a routine to remove commit date when orders on hold
Limited weekday shipments cause orders to ship late	Add memo to customer that pops up when sales order created to remind person creating order

Stock Out Issues

Gaps	Solution
Product quality delayed batch replacement	Purchase material as necessary and dispose of unconsumed quantity (do not store)
Capacity constraints at the "Compounding" work center	Hire and train two more full-time employees to create sufficient capacity
Late discovery of expired items	Add expiration dates to ERP system and proactively remove scrap expired items
Inaccurate inventory	Control Group cycle counting (see below)
New product related issues	See "Breakthrough Process Design" step below

Inventory Accuracy issues

Gaps	Solution
Delayed system receipts	Deliver training to more material handlers to eliminate receipt delays
Discrepancies between ERP and common usage of units of measure for some items	Identify and address discrepancies
Disorganized storage and inventory in multiple overflow areas	Kaizen event (see "Catalyze Success" step below)

Source: Daily Mining

Gaps	Solution
Inadequate scheduling tools and analytics	Redesign scheduling tool to calculate accurate schedule "need" dates
No formal understanding of low schedule attainment	Identify reason for each batch that does not meet need date and perform root cause analysis

New Products Process

Process Redesign Principle: When

Gaps	Solution
Late distribution of bills of material	Develop formal timeline for NPI activities, including BOM distribution and potential change risk to inform purchase decisions
Insufficient knowledge of "Document Control" system	Train purchasing team and add this training to their onboarding
Late forecast availability	Publish forecast at least six months before launch

Process Redesign Principle: Who

Gaps	Solution
Minimal supply agreements with new suppliers causes risk	Hire professional NPI buyer for supplier selection and supply agreement development as needed.; NPI buyer to also perform inventory planning as they will be held accountable for shortages
Inventory planning performed by process engineers	

Process Redesign Principle: What Information

Gaps	Solution
Non-revenue demand sources, such as samples excluded from forecast	Ensure all demand sources are included in the forecast, which would include samples, engineering runs, etc.
No clarity on which forecast version used for supply planning	Assign a version code to every forecast update; forecasts will always include version code when utilized for supply planning
Forecasts tend to be significantly lower than actual demand	Request potential upside opportunities be added to forecast so supply plans can be flexible enough to meet higher end of forecast range

PHASE 3: STEP 2 – CATALYZE SUCCESS

Since inventory was so disorganized throughout the site, we saw it as a terrific opportunity to show the team the power of Kaizen events. In this case, the Kaizen initiative was to improve inventory management, which is a driver for on-time delivery.

As a result of discovery work, we learned that the client had recently installed an expensive Vertical Life Module (VLM). A VLM is a "goods-to-person" picking solution that allows users to pick orders very efficiently while optimizing space utilization within a facility. It is a vertical carousel full of small trays. We learned that the VLM was less than 50% utilized, which presented a big opportunity to remove items from the floor.

The first step was to develop the Kaizen charter. Here are some of the key elements of the charter:

Targets:

➤ Increase warehouse storage capacity by 50%;

➤ Identify and remove 100% of inactive items;

➤ Reduce site overflow inventory from 200pallets to 0 pallets;

Pre-Kaizen activities:

➤ Define "Inactive" criteria. We selected the following criteria:

◆ Excess: More than two years' worth of inventory on hand based upon the greater of recent monthly usage or future monthly MRP (Material Requirements Planning) demand;

◆ Obsolete: No usage in past six months AND no MRP demand;

➤ Excess inventory dollars by item and category;

➤ Redesign warehouse layout to maximize utilization of vertical and floorspace;

➤ Count of overflow inventory by site location (pallets).

Kaizen deliverables:

➤ Inactive items removed from primary warehouse layout;

➤ Storage racks added and configured based upon the redesigned layout;

➤ Remove overflow inventory from overflow locations;

➤ Organize active inventory to maximize storage efficiency;

➤ Inventory strategy for "bulky items."

Actions

1. Move inactive items to trailers stored outside the warehouse;

2. Add and configure new racks;

3. Assess all overflow inventory and categorize as follows:

   a. Smaller items
      These were defined as anything small enough to fit in the VLM, which was approximately 2 x 2 feet, and 3" deep;

   b. Larger items
      Items that were too large for the VLM could either be stored on mobile carts or regular pallet racks. The choice was made based upon the space taken by an item:

      i. Mobile carts: ≤ 5 cases

      ii. Pallet racks > 5 cases

➤ Bulky items (>4 pallets)
Items with more than four pallets on hand were identified for purchasing to assess whether lower levels could be maintained. In addition, we asked that purchasing develop controls to prevent such an inventory buildup in future. Then, based upon average usage per month, we calculated how quickly the excess inventory would "bleed off."

Results:

Once we had defined the criteria for excess and obsolete, we calculated that 43% of items fit within the definition (see table below):

Category	% Total Items
Obsolete items	24%
Items with excess inventory	19%
Total	43%

From an inventory management perspective, this is an excessive amount of unproductive inventory. However, it meant we could transfer a large amount of inventory into the outside containers and make space in the warehouse. Here were some impressive results from the Kaizen:

➤ The Kaizen team installed new racks and existing racks were reconfigured. We also increased pallets from about 44 to 260 pallets;

➤ Every item in an overflow location was manually assessed and moved to the appropriate storage type (VLM, mobile carts, or racks) depending upon the size of the space occupied by the item;

➤ Overflow inventory was reduced from 200 pallet spaces to 0 pallets within three days;

PHASE 3: STEP 3 - OPTIMIZE PORTFOLIO RETURNS

The team determined that the following initiatives would require significant effort, and should be classified as projects:

Source: Gap Discovery

1. *Gap: Material shortages for low demand items. Solution: Make to order*
   It was agreed with the sales team that the inventory strategy for finished goods items with extremely low demand would be changed from "make to stock" (MTS) to "make to order" (MTO). The commitment was that MTS items would be always in stock, but finished goods for MTO items would

only be built as needed for customer orders and given a three-week lead time to allow time for the manufacturing and quality processes. This made sense since an MTS strategy for these low-demand items would highly likely result in continued scrapped inventory as it would not be consumed before it expired.

Source: Breakthrough Process Design

2. *Gap: One supplier per item causing supply risk. Solution: Multi-sourcing*
   It was decided that two suppliers should be qualified for most customized items to minimize supply risk and to leverage competition to improve pricing, quality, and services.

3. *Gap: Engineering develops relationship with supplier with ineffective hand-off to purchasing. Solution: Early purchasing involvement*
   The team agreed that purchasing should be involved in the discussions with suppliers much sooner. While the engineering group is working with the supplier to design the item, the buyer will be discussing commercial arrangements and developing a supply and quality agreement. As discussed earlier, purchasing should be involved earlier and more responsible for the NPI (New Product Introduction) process. They should be negotiating terms and agreements with the suppliers. The buyers should also determine how much to order and when, instead of leaving those decisions to process engineers.

Source: Kaizen event

4. *Gap: Excess inventory of bulky items*
   Solution: Supplier Kanban
   During the Kaizen event, we found that seven active items took up 91 pallet spaces, which was approximately 45% of the total warehouse. When we performed a deeper dive, we found that there was no justification for having so much inventory on hand for these items. For example, the worst offender was the base of a crate used for shipping the final instruments. Its average usage was about 30 bases per month. There were currently 84 bases on hand, or 28 pallets, so only three bases would fit on each pallet.

Since buyers did not trust inventory accuracy, they tended to over-purchase to compensate for the uncertainty. This was not such a large problem for smaller items, but in a space-constrained warehouse, this was most definitely a problem.

Establishing a supplier Kanban meant that there would be tight control on the total inventory either in-transit or in the warehouse. This was a local supplier so total transit time was only 1-2 days. Based upon the recommendations from the ERP system, instead of ordering more bases, Kanban would only trigger replenishments when the physical amount of inventory fell below x number of pallets. Since the usage of bases was about 10 pallets per month with a short transit time, there would be no need to store more than four pallets. This assumed that an agreement was in place with the supplier to always hold inventory at their location, to keep the lead time short. The pallets of bases would be stored together, which would make it easy to see when inventory fell to four pallets. Generally, it is best practice to place a blanket purchase order for an extended amount of time to encourage the supplier to maintain the requested inventory. This would also make the lead time shorter by eliminating time wasted waiting for a purchase order approval. In addition, the material handler, who has constant line of sight of these pallets, should be assigned to call the supplier and request another delivery. In this case, the total space reduction would be from 28 to four pallets, which would take 2-3 months, given the usage of 10 pallets per month. By making these changes for just one item, inventory would be reduced by 24 pallets, or 12% of total inventory.

People

While this was all going on, there were several changes in personnel. It had been obvious from the start that several members of the operations group just did not have the right attitude and we knew they would put a severe drag on the changes that were happening. Several of them were creating a toxic environment by speaking negatively to other team members about the changes taking place. Over the space of about 3-4 months, most of them, seeing the writing on the wall, decided to resign. In other cases, management decided to fire several employees that were seen as obstacles to making necessary changes. As each of the naysayers left, the reduction in resistance was palpable. Before they left, it felt like identifying opportunities for improvement was a small piece of the puzzle, and persuading the incumbents was by far the largest challenge. Even if the change was accepted, the least amount of effort possible was put into it, so progress was at a snail's pace. The biggest issue, though, was that each of the improvements always takes a few cycles of gradual improvement and attention to detail before reaching their full potential. Without this level of focus, the improvement will never meet its full potential and will likely not develop enough momentum to be successful. However, we also found several employees that recognized that things needed to change and actively welcomed it.

CONCLUSION

With all the changes discussed in this case study, we completely turned around the client's supply chain to consistently achieve on-time delivery within four months. Where on-time shipping performance had been less than 70% when we started, it is now consistently above 90%. We achieved this by bringing clarity to the questions below so that the team could make calculated decisions, and would know what actions to take so results would continuously improve:

➤ When do we really need the purchase order?

➤ How much revenue is at risk for the quarter?

➤ When do we really need the production order?

➤ How accurate is the sales forecast, offset by six months to allow for the lead time of many buy items?

➤ What can we really manufacture given material shortages?

➤ What are the critical few reasons for shipping customer orders late?

➤ How does manufacturing capacity by work center compare to current and future needs?

> ➤ Which instrument parts need to be allocated between field service and instrument production, and what is that allocation?

> ➤ Which inventory will expire before production consumes it so that we can plan for it?

> ➤ What are the steps of each operational process i.e., purchasing, receiving, quality testing, planning, scheduling, inventory management, manufacturing, shipping etc., and who is responsible for each step?

Parting Words

I hope that you have found this book informative. My hope is that it will change the way you and your organization think, period. Having practiced this approach for more than 20 years, it has become second nature to me. Whenever I am confronted with undesirable results, my mind instantly thinks: which process, where in the process, and what could solve the problem? For example, if the client tells me that they frequently make shipping errors, I don't automatically think about which person is screwing up; I assume that the mistake is due to a process gap. While it could be that the person is not the best-performing employee, it does not matter. Your business processes should be designed with a lower-performing employee in mind, not the best. Think about it: each step of your business process cannot always be operated by top employees. The design should be robust enough to withstand normal, expected human error.

This approach will mean that problems are defined better, investigated more effectively, and addressed more quickly. You will consistently meet your strategic objectives because you much better understand what precisely is required without relying upon opinions. Your organization will be able to better track progress to your strategic objectives.

Another reason you will meet your strategic objectives more effectively is because your projects will be much more closely aligned with these objectives. Your projects will also be executed much more effectively, and using Kaizen events where possible, they will be completed much more rapidly.

Good luck in your transformation efforts and be sure to contact me if you have any questions.

After obtaining his BS in Biochemistry at the University of Sheffield, England and an MBA from CSU East Bay, Steve has become a leading expert in life science supply chain management and operational excellence. He has APICS and Lean Six Sigma Black Belt certifications and has taught these courses to students for 20+ years.

Steve has over 25 years' experience with notable life science companies, such as Danaher Corporation, Bio-Rad Laboratories, Santen Inc, BioMarin Pharmaceutical, and Bio-Techne, as well as smaller start-up organizations. Over the years, he has developed an unparalleled reputation for his structured approach, tenacity, and his ability to consistently deliver results.

Steve is the founder of BioSupply Consulting LLC, helping life science clients transform their supply chain capability and performance. He has been the guest speaker at several APICS events and supply chain related podcasts. He also publishes a weekly newsletter to his 16K LinkedIn followers.

If you would like to learn more about how to quickly and sustainably transform supply chain performance for your patients, customers, and other stakeholders, please email Steve at steve@biosupplyconsulting.com, or check out at biosupplyconsulting.com.

Mine the Gaps

www.ingramcontent.com/pod-product-compliance
Lightning Source LLC
LaVergne TN
LVHW051249080426
835513LV00016B/1821